Library of Congress Cataloging-in-Publication Data available.
ISBN: 978-0-8118-7486-1

Manufactured in China

Design by Catherine Grishaver
Art Direction by Anne Donnard
Cover Design by Vanessa Dina
Full-page food styling by Jamie Kimm
Full-page prop styling by Marina Malchin

The recipes included in this book have been re-created from live cooking
events on the *Top Chef* television series with some modifications for the home
cook. The information in this book has been researched and tested, and all
efforts have been made to ensure accuracy. Neither the publisher nor the
creators can assume responsibility for any accident, injuries, losses, or other
damages resulting from the use of this book.

Photographs, except all full-page food photographs, are courtesy of
Bravo Media, LLC.

Top Chef and Bravo are trademarks of Bravo Media, a division of NBC Universal.

Activa TG-RM is a registered trademark of Ajinomoto Kabushiki Kaisha DBA Ajinomoto Co., Inc.;
Cheetos Flamin' Hot and Fritos are registered trademarks of Frito-Lay North America, Inc.;
CornNuts is a registered trademark of Kraft Foods Global, Inc.; Dr Pepper is a registered trademark
of Dr Pepper/Seven Up, Inc.; Goldschläger is a registered trademark of Diageo plc.; Maldon Sea Salt
is a registered trademark of Maldon Crystal Salt Company Ltd.; Rodenbach Grand Cru is a registered
trademark of Palm Breweries Joint Stock Company; Silpat is a registered trademark of Demarle Inc.,
USA; Wondra is a registered trademark of General Mills, Inc.

10 9 8 7 6 5 4 3 2 1

Chronicle Books LLC
680 Second Street
San Francisco, California 94107
www.chroniclebooks.com

HOW TO COOK LIKE A
TOPCHEF

FOREWORD BY **RICK BAYLESS**
TEXT BY **EMILY MILLER**
PHOTOGRAPHS BY **ANTONIS ACHILLEOS**

CHRONICLE BOOKS
SAN FRANCISCO

table of contents

kitchen fundamentals:
sides, soups, salads, starches

principles of protein:
beef, lamb, pork, poultry

seafood essentials: scallops to ceviche

foreign exchange: cooking with global flavors

advanced culinary applications: Top Chef extreme

last course: the art of dessert

TOP CHEF MASTER FOREWORD

I guess I am lucky. My childhood memories are a glorious grab bag of dicing, slicing, roasting, deep-frying, smoking, simmering—everything that went on in the prep kitchen of my parents' Oklahoma City barbecue restaurant in the '50s and '60s.

Some folks might think a professional kitchen is no place for a kid to grow up. I mean, think about it: 500-degree ovens, 375-degree oil, slippery floors, an arsenal of knives dangling through wooden slots on the side of a prep table, just about level with a five-year-old's head. But for me, that kitchen was a wonderland, and all the cooks knew that's how I felt. So they took that little boy into their fold. They taught me what every good cook—and Top Chef—has to master: a respect for the tools of the trade. A respect that allows one to utilize those tools to their greatest potential, with intimate understanding and without fear.

That's how I learned to roast some meats at high temperatures, smoke others at low ones, fearlessly reach a short pair of tongs into boiling oil to retrieve a golden this or that, dice a gallon of celery in a matter of moments, scrub a burnt pot until no trace of waywardness remains . . . all essential techniques learned so long ago they now seem more akin to intuition than a curriculum I once had to master by sheer repetition.

Smack-dab in the middle of those years, Julia Child started making her famous "French Chef" cooking shows for public television—and my world changed. She revealed to me techniques and flavors and preparations that transcended the repertory of my family's restaurant. She introduced me to all kinds of equipment and remarkable things to do with a chicken or a piece of pie crust. No longer could I satisfy my nearly unquenchable kitchen thirst solely at the Hickory House on Oklahoma City's southwest side. But this time I didn't have a bunch of professional cooks to show me the intricacies and finesse of the new techniques I wanted to master—only a single cookbook and a once-a-week TV show.

Now, unless your family has its own Julia, chances are you're living with a cookbooks-and-TV culinary education, too. This needn't be a discouragement, as long as you don't mind spending enough time in the kitchen for those techniques to migrate from the brain to the fingers: to become second nature. I'm sure that's what Jacques Pépin, the French technique master widely known from his television shows and books, was getting at when, as a budding young chef, I asked him where I should go for culinary education. Without a word, he pointed at the stove in the small kitchen where I'd prepared his lunch.

Nothing beats practice, especially when television and the Internet can provide masterful demonstrations at the click of a button. Practice, plus a mind that's open and adventurous. After growing up in a meat-centric barbecue restaurant, I immersed myself in Julia's French kitchen, and then later fell head over heels in love with a plate of chicken *mole*—which led to my learning a brand-new set of techniques.

That's when the lightbulb went off: techniques are all we cooks have for transforming beautiful ingredients into seductive, thrilling, memorable flavors and textures. If recipes are the sheet music of our kitchens, then mastered techniques are our way of making them sing.

Funny thing is, you can discover amazing techniques in the most unlikely places. I learned to make Mexico's most complex sauce, Oaxacan black *mole*, from an old woman cooking in clay pots over

BY RICK BAYLESS
Winner of **TOP CHEF Masters**, Season 1

an open fire, at a little ranch in the middle of nowhere. Still, it took me ten years to master what she showed me in a single afternoon—to be able to create a flavor that captured hearts like hers did. I don't know why it took me so long to figure out that the point of great technique isn't just refinement or intricacy or dazzle. It's incredible flavor. Well, incredible flavor and haunting texture; in my mind, they're intertwined. Both taste and texture can take you to new and unexpected levels of pleasure and appreciation.

Being a great chef or a Top Chef isn't necessarily about this-or-that culinary school—although I am a staunch believer in young chefs going to school to learn the language and essential techniques of the professional kitchen. A great chef is born from dedication to searching out awe-inspiring tastes and textures, then putting in the hours to master the techniques that created them.

I leave you aspiring Top Chefs with two recommendations: first, become friends with fire. From scarcely perceivable to aggressive, the right heat—even when "right" means "intense"—is one of the most important techniques you'll ever master. And second, dedicate yourself to your knives. Keeping them razor-sharp is essential to ease, accomplishment, and, of course, safety (since dull knives account for far more kitchen accidents than sharp ones).

Wait, there's a third: trust your taste buds. That's what'll get you furthest as you strive for Top Chef-dom.

INTRODUCTION

Want to learn how to make Stefan's Roasted Duck or Hubert Keller's Mac and Cheese (with or without a dorm shower)? Are you curious about how Jennifer C. prepares her mussels, or what goes into Rick Bayless's guacamoles? *How to Cook like a Top Chef* not only gives you the recipes, it also teaches you the fundamental techniques that make these dishes work.

How to Cook like a Top Chef takes a deeper look at the skills and techniques behind the dishes made in the *Top Chef* kitchen. It provides a road map, a distillation of tips, tricks, and insider knowledge that will make you a better and smarter cook. It's the ultimate *Top Chef* bible. In these pages, Jamie walks us through her process for perfectly searing scallops; Fabio gives us step-by-step tips for turning out fabulous fresh pasta; and Kevin shares his passion for pork.

Top Chef is a reality TV show, a cooking competition that entertains us and keeps us glued to the edge of our seats. Who will create a culinary masterpiece and win over the judges? Who will have a meltdown and end up in tears before the hour is through?

In between the drama and the tension, we are watching something very exciting taking place: seasoned professionals and talented rookies performing at the top of their game. *Top Chef* has given us the opportunity to go deep into the kitchen and watch how chefs really work. Okay, maybe most chefs don't create their menu by rolling dice or prepare fine food over a faulty hot plate in their living room, but real chefs have to think on their feet. No matter the circumstances or behind-the-scenes disasters, diners expect them to turn out extraordinary food, using all their technical skill, creativity, and culinary know-how.

Every season, a group of fresh new chef'testants arrives at the *Top Chef* kitchen, whites ironed, knives sharpened, ready to do battle. Season 6 in Las Vegas began with the famed Mise-en-

Place Relay Race Quickfire Challenge, which set the tone for some very stiff competition. This was a not-so-subtle reminder: it doesn't matter who you've worked for, what your diploma says, or how vast your tattoo gallery—if you don't have your core skills up to snuff, you're not going to make it here.

Each season has upped the ante, from the creativity of the challenges to the caliber of the chef'testants. Selling tacos from a street cart has given way to cooking over fire pits in the middle of the desert, surrounded by rattlesnakes and hungry ranchers. We've watched chefs wrangle with octopuses, alligators, snails, and cacti. They've catered weddings, opened restaurants, and made Thanksgiving dinner for the Foo Fighters. They've had to serve fish to Eric Ripert, gumbo to Emeril, and *sauce béarnaise* to Joël Robuchon.

Even on *Top Chef Masters*, where many of the chefs competing are accustomed to a small army of assistants, sous-chefs, and line cooks, the skills learned over a lifetime came through loud and clear. Even though at the top of their game, when asked to do mundane tasks such as shucking oysters, dressing chickens, or whipping egg whites, chefs like Anita Lo, Art Smith, and Hubert Keller did not demur; that's because the same techniques learned early on come into play every single day in a professional kitchen. Whether asked to serve appetizers to one hundred hungry guests with no help or coax real flavor out of vegan ingredients, chefs such as Michael Chiarello and Rick Moonen rose to the challenge over and over again.

Top Chef has become a showcase for creative and innovative cooks, from the impresarios of Asian, Mexican, Italian, and French cuisine featured on *Top Chef Masters* to the innovative chef'testants who use chemicals and avant-garde techniques to take their dishes to a whole new level. Even the words "Top Chef" can now be used as an adjective to describe the sexing up of home cooking: e.g., "Honey, I went all Top Chef on the roast tonight and made a sunchoke *gastrique* to go with it."

The show has made dinner parties into a competitive sport, inspiring us to try unusual new ingredients, and encouraging us to take more chances and have more fun in the kitchen. In essence, it has inspired us to think more like Top Chefs and to cook outside the box.

KITCHEN FUNDAMENTALS: SIDES, SOUPS, SALADS, STARCHES

15

25

37

39

21

SLICING & DICING

Chopping onions, mincing parsley . . . it may sound banal, but tasks like these are the foundation of cooking. From the Mise-en-Place Relays to the apple brunoise contest on the first episode of Season 5, we've seen again and again how core skills form the backbone of any great chef. To make paper-thin slices, as well as some decorative cuts, you may need a mandoline. Otherwise, a sharp knife will do the job.

CHOPPING

The most important thing when chopping vegetables for a mirepoix (a mixture of diced onion, carrot, and celery) or other preparations is to make the cuts roughly the same size so the vegetables will cook evenly. Relish your uniform cuts by making Rick Bayless's Chips and Salsa (page 127).

When chopping onions, peel the onion and cut it in half through the root. Lay the flat side on the cutting board and make 2 or 3 horizontal cuts toward, but not all the way through, the root end.

Then make evenly spaced vertical cuts all along the onion half, still stopping just short of the root end.

Finally, make a series of crosswise cuts—that is, perpendicular to the vertical cuts—closely spaced to make even pieces of the desired size.

MINCING

Mincing is a finer cut, typically used for fresh herbs, garlic, and shallots. When mincing herbs, first handpick the leaves from the stems; gather them in a pile on your cutting board; and make a series of quick, shallow cuts, keeping the tip of the knife in contact with the board while you rock the handle up and down. Gather the herbs again and repeat, from another direction, as many times as you need to until you have a fine mince. Practice mincing when assembling Hector's Tofu Ceviche (page 128).

CHIFFONADE

Chiffonade, the chef's term for shredding, is usually used for leafy herbs such as basil and mint, but also works for larger-leafed greens such as chard and kale, once you remove the stalks. To cut a chiffonade, neatly stack the stemmed leaves on top of one another; curl or roll them lengthwise, then slice them crosswise into thin slivers. This skill is needed in Carla's Crab–Shiso Soup (page 121).

JULIENNE

To make this neat, rectangular cut, first you need to square off the vegetable. Cut the pieces lengthwise into little planks, then stack these up and slice again lengthwise, then crosswise in half or into thirds, if desired, to create uniform little match-sticks. Mike I.'s Tuna, Pears, and Ponzu (page 135) gets its texture from a neat julienne.

BRUNOISE

A brunoise cut results in a small, neat dice of perfect cubes. Start by cutting your carrots, apples, or potatoes into a neat julienne (above), then chop them into uniform little cubes to make a brunoise. Try this technique on Eli's Clam Chowder (page 29).

ARIANE'S TOMATO, WATERMELON, AND FETA SALAD

WINNER!

BASIL OIL

Leaves from 1 bunch fresh basil

1/2 cup olive oil

Salt

SALAD

3 large, ripe tomatoes (about 2 pounds), preferably beefsteak, cored and each cut into 4 thick slices

Seedless watermelon, cut into twelve 3-inch-long batons

About 8 ounces firm sheep's-milk feta cheese, cut into eight 2-inch-long batons

GARNISH

1/4 cup aged balsamic vinegar

Herbed fleur de sel for serving

Small fresh basil leaves

SERVES 4

FOR THE BASIL OIL: Bring a saucepan of water to a boil and have a bowl of ice water ready. Blanch and shock the basil. Drain well and squeeze the basil to remove as much water as possible. Transfer the basil to a blender. Add the olive oil and a generous sprinkling of salt, then blend to a smooth purée, about 1 minute. Strain the basil oil through a fine-mesh sieve into a small bowl. Set aside.

FOR THE SALAD: Place 3 slices of tomato on each of 4 salad plates. Top the tomato with 3 pieces of watermelon and 2 pieces of feta cheese per plate.

FOR THE GARNISH: Drizzle each salad with the vinegar and 1 tablespoon of the basil oil. Place a small spoon filled with fleur de sel on the side of each plate. Garnish with the small basil leaves and serve. (The remaining basil oil will keep in an airtight container in the refrigerator for up to 1 week.)

Prep time: 20 minutes

Season 5, Episode 4

Elimination Challenge:
Create a dish to be cooked and served for a 2½-minute live TV presentation.

ABOUT A TECHNIQUE

blanch and shock

To *blanch* is to plunge a food into boiling water for a short interval of 30 seconds to 5 minutes. This method pre-cooks foods that will be used in additional preparation. After boiling, you plunge the food into ice water to shock it and arrest cooking.

To blanch and shock: Bring a pot of salted water to a boil. Prepare a large bowl of ice water and put out a strainer. Wash and trim your food. When the water has reached a full boil, add the food and cook for about 2 minutes. Strain immediately and plunge into ice water for at least 10 minutes.

"I've been making this salad forever. It's something that looks and tastes great, and that anyone can do at home."

ARIANE, SEASON 5

Q + A

gail simmons

With her warm smile and wise comments, Gail Simmons is the friendly face at Judges' Table. Between Padma's worldly sophistication and Tom's no-nonsense expertise, Gail provides the perspective of a down-to-earth diner eating these dishes and then handing out educated, yet compassionate decisions about the chef'testants' fates. First cooking school, then stints in top New York kitchens and time working with food writer Jeffrey Steingarten and chef-impresario Daniel Boulud provided Gail with the background for her starring roles as Special Projects Director at *Food & Wine* magazine and judge on *Top Chef*.

How is your role as a judge different from Padma's or Tom's?

I think of my place on the show as the diner. Padma is the host. Tom is the chef; he goes into the kitchen, chats with the chefs, sees how things are going. I come at it like a diner in a restaurant because all I know to judge them on is what I see in front of me on the plate.

Do you think it's fair to judge chefs by their work under such stressful circumstances?

Working in a restaurant is totally insane, so if anyone is capable of surviving in a stressful, challenging atmosphere and handling curveballs thrown at them it's a chef. Everyone on the show is in the same position. They've had the same amount of sleep, the same campfire stove, no access to TVs or recipes—they're all quarantined. We want to see if these chefs can think (and cook) on their feet.

How do you work out who will be eliminated at Judges' Table?

When we talk to the chef'testants at Judges' Table, we go through each dish individually on both the top and bottom. Most of the time we don't know who will be eliminated when we start

out. The discussion is very extensive, much more so than what's shown on TV, especially for the chefs on the bottom. We want to really find out the backstory of what went wrong and whether they understand that they did something wrong. If it's a team, we want to know who was responsible for what.

What if the judges don't agree?

In the end, we can't have a disagreement. The decision needs to be unanimous, so we hash it out at length and talk it over, and that's where Judges' Table takes time. The finales are the most difficult because we often cannot decide who should be the winner. That's when we end up at Judges' Table until 6 or 7 in the morning. But we're in it together. If we're in some kind of a deadlock, if one person disagrees, you need to convince them.

Can you usually predict the winner early on?

I can tell you within the first two episodes who the best chefs are, but that doesn't mean they're going to make it to the finale. Every challenge is judged individually, so a talented chef can have one bad day and be out. Probably the best example of this was Tre from Season 3. He was definitely in the top four in terms of talent, but he was the leader of his team for Restaurant Wars, he messed up that day, and that's it. Richard B. and

Stefan were both front-runners going into the finales, and both sort of choked.

So it's a game, just like baseball. The Yankees are the best team in the league, with the most talented and highly paid players, but they don't win the World Series every year because a million different things can happen.

Is it ever tempting to judge cumulatively instead of challenge by challenge?

We are constantly reminded by one another, and by the producers, that we really are looking at each dish, not at the person. Tom is a stickler for detail and for truth, so he keeps us all on the straight and narrow. The guest judges also play such an important part: they don't know these people, they've never eaten their food before, and they're totally objective.

Who have been your favorite guest judges?

That's a hard one because we've had so many amazing people. Eric Ripert, Daniel Boulud—he is such a mentor of mine. Natalie Portman was really awesome; she has a real interest in food. Tim Love was a blast.

What have been some of your favorite challenges?

I like the ones that get the chef'testants out of the kitchen, out of their normal environment. I loved the challenge in Season 1 when they had to cook and serve from street carts in the Mission district in San Francisco. In New York, of course the Elimination Challenge where the chef'testants catered my bridal shower was my favorite. In Season 6 we did a lot of stuff at other locations; my favorite was the challenge at the air force base. It was really emotional and exciting.

What was the *Top Chef Masters* Season 1 finale like?

It was by far the best finale food we have ever eaten. It felt like it should have been illegal. Each one of the chefs was exceptional, and each surprised me. We were all in awe of them.

How can you all eat that much food at one sitting?

This is our job, so we learn to taste and to have restraint, even though sometimes it's so delicious you want to eat the whole thing. And then I go for a long run in the morning.

SUZANNE TRACHT'S FRIED SHALLOT RINGS

AÏOLI

One 12-ounce can Dr Pepper

1 egg yolk

1/2 cup canola oil

1/2 cup extra-virgin olive oil

1 teaspoon fresh lemon juice

1 or 2 strips beef jerky, minced

1/2 cup mixed fresh herb leaves, such as basil and mint, julienned

....

FRIED SHALLOT RINGS

11/2 cups buttermilk

Salt and freshly ground pepper

6 shallots, sliced into rings

1/2 cup rice flour

1/2 cup all-purpose flour

One 1-ounce bag Cheetos Flamin' Hot, finely ground with a pinch of fleur de sel

One 1-ounce bag Fritos, finely ground

1 teaspoon spicy beef soup mix

Canola oil for deep-frying

⊘ **Prep time:** 30 minutes

▭ *Top Chef Masters*, Season 1, Episode 2

🔥 Quickfire Challenge: Create an *amuse-bouche* using ingredients found in a vending machine.

SERVES 2

FOR THE AÏOLI: In a small saucepan, simmer the Dr Pepper over medium-high heat until reduced by half and thickened to a syrup, about 5 minutes. Remove from the heat and set aside to cool.

Whisk the egg yolk in a medium bowl. Combine the oils and add to the egg yolk in a slow, thin stream, whisking constantly, until the mixture thickens to the consistency of a loose mayonnaise. Whisk the Dr Pepper syrup into the mixture, then stir in the lemon juice, jerky, and herbs. Cover and refrigerate until ready to serve. (The aïoli must be used within 10 hours.)

FOR THE FRIED SHALLOT RINGS: In a medium bowl, combine the buttermilk and a couple of pinches of salt and pepper. Separate the shallot rings.

In another bowl, mix together the flours, ground Cheetos and Fritos, and soup mix.

Line a baking sheet with paper towels. Pour about 3 inches of oil into a deep, heavy-bottomed saucepan and heat over medium-high heat to 325°F on a deep-frying thermometer. Remove the shallot rings from the buttermilk and dredge them in the flour mixture, shaking off any excess. Carefully add the coated rings to the hot oil, working in batches as needed to avoid crowding, and fry until crisp and golden brown, about 2 minutes. Remove the rings with a slotted spoon and drain on the paper towel–lined baking sheet. Season with salt. If frying in batches, hold the fried rings in a warm (200°F) oven while you cook the rest.

To serve, place the shallot rings on a plate with the aïoli on the side.

What's
HOT & NOT
What's NOT

Because of the concentration of young, talented chefs gathered under one roof, the *Top Chef* kitchen has become a kind of laboratory for what's happening in restaurants around the country—from cooking with liquid nitrogen to rediscovering regional comfort foods. Our chef'testants weigh in on what's fresh and what's tired in our current food-obsessed culture.

BACK TO BASICS
"I want food that looks like food, so I'm returning to a much simpler style of cuisine."
—LEE ANNE, SEASON 1

FAMILY STYLE
"Sharing family style is big. Everyone gets different dishes and shares, so your palate is refreshed with various textures, flavors, aromas."
—MARCEL, SEASON 2

SMALL FOOD
"People like small bites they can pop in their mouth. I make these mini ice-cream sandwiches that everyone goes crazy for."
—CARLA, SEASON 5

MOLECULAR MAGIC
"Liquid nitrogen is becoming mainstream. You can make sorbet in minutes, make ice cream at the table, and there's a big *wow* factor."
—HOSEA, SEASON 5

FOOD AS THEATER
"I don't need to see any more foam or smoke. Food is about substance and energy; it doesn't need to be so theatrical."
—SPIKE, SEASON 4

CHARCUTERIE
"I don't need to see another charcuterie plate."
—RICHARD B., SEASON 4

FANCY DINING
"The whole fine dining thing is falling by the wayside."
—MARCEL, SEASON 2

CHEF'S TASTING MARATHON
"The three-and-a-half-hour, fifteen-course meal is over. I want a slice of pizza after I finish! I'm over it."
—NIKKI, SEASON 4

JEFF'S FRIED GREEN TOMATOES

7 large, firm green tomatoes

Salt and freshly ground pepper

5 eggs

1/2 cup water

1 1/2 cups all-purpose flour

2 1/2 cups panko bread crumbs

Olive oil for frying

Red Tomato Jam (below) for serving

SERVES 8

Cut the tomatoes crosswise into 1/2-inch-thick slices, sprinkle with about 1 table-spoon each salt and pepper, and set aside.

Beat the eggs with the water in a medium bowl. Combine the flour with a generous sprinkling of salt and pepper in a shallow dish. Put the panko in another shallow dish.

Dredge each of the tomato slices in the seasoned flour, shaking off any excess. Dip them in the egg wash, then dredge them in the bread crumbs.

Line 2 baking sheets with paper towels. In a heavy skillet, heat about 1/2 inch olive oil over medium-high heat until shimmering. Add the tomato slices, in batches as needed to avoid crowding, and fry, turning once, until golden brown and crispy, about 3 minutes total. Add more olive oil as necessary. Transfer the cooked slices to the paper towel–lined baking sheets. Blot dry and let drain.

To serve, place the warm tomato slices on a plate with the tomato jam.

🕐 **Prep time:** 30 minutes

🖥 **Season 5, Episode 8**

🔪 **Elimination Challenge:**
Create a seasonal lunch using fresh ingredients from a farm.

HOW TO MAKE
red tomato jam

6 large, red heirloom tomatoes, blanched, peeled, and seeded

2 tablespoons olive oil

1 teaspoon sea salt

Chop the tomatoes and combine with the olive oil and salt in a sauté pan over low heat. Cook until the tomatoes break down and concentrate into jam, about 25 minutes. Let cool before using.

> "When you're out on the farm you really try to use everything that's available, so I picked up those green tomatoes and fried them up."
>
> JEFF, SEASON 5

Q + A

WITH
lee anne

Talented chef Lee Anne Wong just missed making it to the finale in Season 1. That was only the beginning of her *Top Chef* experience, however, as she was later hired by the producers to be the show's supervising culinary producer. A veteran of the French Culinary Institute in New York and the woman behind *Wong Way to Cook*, a webisode series featured on www.bravotv.com, Lee Anne fills us in on what happens on the *Top Chef* set.

What do your *Top Chef* duties entail?
It's a long list that includes developing challenges with the segment producers and executives, building and maintaining the pantry, scouting locations, sourcing ingredients, setting up challenges, and managing the still photos of finished dishes (a.k.a food porn). I also do cleanup, the least glamorous part of the job. The chef'testants like me because I do their dishes.

How have you developed the *Top Chef* kitchen?
I've spent the past several years trying to build the ultimate kitchen. It took the newest baby, *Top Chef Masters*, to convince the higher-ups that I needed to build a tech corner. It was amusing because some chefs, like Jonathan Waxman, would glance over at it, snort, and walk in the other direction, while others, such as Michael Cimarusti, Wylie Dufresne, and Nils Noren, were quite stunned at the fact that they had absolutely everything they could need. Blais and Marcel would have enjoyed cooking in this kitchen very much.

You help develop the Quickfire Challenges and Elimination Challenges. What are the criteria for challenges that end up on the show?
I often think about what I go through as a chef and the aspects of the business beyond just cooking, such as teamwork, problem solving, and being able to adapt when the game changes (what we call "the twist"). At the end of the day, I put myself in the chef'testants' shoes and think about how I would handle the challenge and if it's viable. It's also my job to make sure the chef'testants aren't set up for failure.

What goes on behind the scenes of the *Top Chef* kitchen that would surprise viewers?
Me cooking massive dinners out of my hotel room for the crew using only a toaster oven and microwave. No really. Ask the lighting department.

What is your advice for future chef'testants?
First, keep your head on straight. *Top Chef* is a tremendous opportunity to learn about yourself as a chef and person. Second, there is life after *Top Chef*. Keep it real and know that *Top Chef* is a stepping-stone and a means to advance your career, but at the end of the day you still need to be a good chef and run your business. Trust me, there's another season coming right behind you.

What's your cooking motto?
At least half of cooking is intuition and common sense: If you smell something burning, it's probably burning.

JAMIE'S GRILLED CORN SALAD

CORN SALAD

8 ears corn, roasted in their husks on a grill or in the oven, then shucked

1 red bell pepper, seeded and cut into brunoise

1 orange bell pepper, seeded and cut into brunoise

1 green bell pepper, seeded and cut into brunoise

1 small red onion, cut into brunoise

Leaves from 1/2 bunch fresh basil, cut into chiffonade

Leaves from 1/2 bunch fresh flat-leaf parsley, cut into chiffonade

1/4 to 1/2 cup white wine vinegar

3/4 cup extra-virgin olive oil

Salt

DRESSING

2 tablespoons water

1 clove garlic

1 English cucumber, cut into large dice

Leaves from 1/2 bunch fresh dill, coarsely chopped

1 1/2 cups sour cream

About 2 tablespoons cider vinegar

Salt and freshly ground pepper

SERVES 4 TO 6

FOR THE SALAD: Cut the kernels off the corn cobs and combine in a large bowl with the bell peppers, onion, basil, parsley, 1/4 cup wine vinegar, and the olive oil. Season with salt, taste, and adjust the flavor with a little more vinegar if needed. Refrigerate until ready to serve.

FOR THE DRESSING: In a blender or food processor, combine the water, garlic, and cucumber. Blend until smooth. Add the dill and blend until well combined. Put the sour cream in a medium bowl and whisk in the cucumber mixture. Season with cider vinegar, salt, and pepper. Refrigerate until ready to serve.

To serve, toss the corn salad with about two-thirds of the dressing. Drizzle with additional dressing as desired.

Prep time: 40 minutes, plus 30 minutes for roasting corn

Season 5, Episode 3

Elimination Challenge: Make Thanksgiving dinner for the rock band Foo Fighters.

"I love corn. You can eat it raw or cooked, purée it or turn it into a sauce, make a corn flan or pudding. It can be savory or sweet."

JAMIE, SEASON 5

BRYAN'S MACARONS WITH GUACAMOLE

WINNER!

MACARONS

4 egg whites

1 1/2 teaspoons cream of tartar

Grated zest of 1 lime

1/2 cup sugar

. . . .

GUACAMOLE

2 ripe avocados, pitted, peeled, and cut into large dice

1 teaspoon fresh lime juice

1/2 teaspoon red wine vinegar

1 1/2 teaspoons ground cumin

1/4 cup minced red onion

1 jalapeño chile, seeded and minced

2 tablespoons finely chopped fresh cilantro

Salt and freshly ground pepper

CORN PURÉE

1 tablespoon unsalted butter

1 stalk lemongrass, smashed

1 kaffir lime leaf

1 cup fresh or frozen corn kernels

3 sprigs fresh cilantro

Salt and freshly ground pepper

1 cup heavy cream

. . . .

1/4 cup CornNuts, finely ground

MAKES 40 MACARONS

FOR THE MACARONS: Preheat the oven to 185°F. Line 2 baking sheets with parchment paper. Combine the egg whites, cream of tartar, and lime zest in a bowl. Using an electric mixer, beat on high speed until soft peaks form. Add the sugar a little at a time, beating well after each addition. Continue to whip until the whites are stiff and glossy. Transfer to a pastry bag fitted with a medium round tip or plastic bag with the corner cut off and pipe small round domes of meringue about 2 inches in diameter onto the prepared baking sheet. Bake until a pale golden brown and dry to the touch, 2 1/2 to 3 hours. If it's a humid day, you may need to turn off the oven and let the *macarons* dry for up to 12 hours. Set aside to cool completely.

FOR THE GUACAMOLE: Combine the avocados, lime juice, vinegar, and cumin in a food processor and process until smooth. Transfer to a medium bowl and stir in the onion, jalapeño, and cilantro. Season with salt and pepper. Scoop the guacamole into a pastry bag fitted with a small round tip or a plastic bag and set aside in the refrigerator.

FOR THE CORN PURÉE: Melt the butter in a sauté pan over medium-high heat. Add the lemongrass and lime leaf and sweat until soft. Add the corn kernels and cilantro and sweat for 10 minutes longer. Season with salt and pepper. Stir in the cream and simmer for about 10 minutes. Remove the lemongrass, lime leaf, and cilantro and transfer the corn mixture to a blender. Blend until smooth, then pass the purée through a fine-mesh sieve. Set aside.

To serve, pipe the guacamole between 2 *macarons*. Spoon small circles of corn purée onto a plate or plates and set a *macaron* sandwich on top of each pool of purée. Dust the plate with the CornNuts and serve.

Prep time: 45 minutes, plus 3 hours for baking

Season 6, Episode 2

Elimination Challenge: Cater a bachelor/bachelorette party in two teams split by gender.

BRYAN DISHES

"The *macaron* is something that I use at my restaurant a lot. The idea is to create a very light-flavored shell that is crisp, so layers of texture can be achieved with a smooth purée or pudding. Normally in the mid Atlantic it takes about ten hours to prepare these *macarons* using a dehydrator; I took a huge risk trying to pull this off. I relied on the environment, being in the desert, to dry the *macarons* overnight."

KEVIN'S MUSHROOMS WITH TARRAGON-PISTACHIO PESTO

TARRAGON-PISTACHIO PESTO

Leaves from 2 bunches fresh flat-leaf parsley

1/2 cup fresh tarragon leaves

1/4 cup unsalted raw pistachios

2 to 3 tablespoons extra-virgin olive oil

Salt and freshly ground pepper

BRAISED MORELS

1/2 tablespoon water

2 tablespoons cold unsalted butter, cubed

Salt

1 cup fresh morel mushrooms, brushed clean and halved lengthwise, or dried morels, reconstituted

Fresh lemon juice

SAUTÉED MUSHROOMS

1 tablespoon canola oil

1 teaspoon unsalted butter

3 cups fresh hen of the woods mushrooms, brushed clean and sliced

1 rib celery, finely diced

Grated zest and juice of 1/2 lemon

Salt and freshly ground pepper

TURNIP PURÉE

Salt

1 medium turnip, peeled and thinly sliced

2 tablespoons heavy cream

4 tablespoons unsalted butter, at room temperature

1 teaspoon sugar

PAN-SEARED KALE

1 tablespoon cider vinegar

1 teaspoon water

1 tablespoon olive oil

2 bunches kale, stemmed

1 onion, diced

1 clove garlic, minced

1/2 teaspoon red pepper flakes

Salt

🕐 Prep time: 1 hour

🖥 Season 6, Episode 10

🔪 Elimination Challenge: Prepare a vegetarian dish for Natalie Portman.

SERVES 4 TO 6 AS AN APPETIZER

FOR THE TARRAGON-PISTACHIO PESTO: In a food processor, combine the parsley, tarragon, and pistachios. With the motor running, drizzle in 2 tablespoons olive oil and process until smooth and well combined. Add additional olive oil if a thinner consistency is desired. Season to taste with salt and pepper.

FOR THE BRAISED MORELS: In a small saucepan, bring the water to a boil over medium-high heat. Reduce the heat to low and whisk in the butter, a few pieces at a time, until the butter is melted and fully emulsified. Season to taste with salt. Add the morels and braise in the *beurre monté* until tender, 5 to 10 minutes. Remove from the heat and season to taste with lemon juice. Cover and set aside.

FOR THE SAUTÉED MUSHROOMS: In a medium sauté pan, heat the oil over medium-high heat. Melt the butter in the oil until lightly browned, then add the mushrooms. Sauté the mushrooms until golden brown and tender, 5 to 10 minutes. Add the celery and sauté for 1 minute longer. Stir in the lemon zest and juice. Season to taste with salt and pepper. Cover and set aside.

FOR THE TURNIP PURÉE: Bring a small pot of water to a boil over high heat and salt it lightly. Add turnip slices, reduce the heat to medium, and simmer, partially covered, until tender, 5 to 10 minutes. Drain the turnip, reserving the water. Combine the turnip and cream in a blender and purée until smooth. Add the reserved cooking water, a little at a time, if a thinner consistency is desired. Transfer the purée to a bowl and stir in the butter. Season with the sugar and salt to taste. Cover and set aside.

FOR THE KALE: In a small bowl, combine the vinegar and water. Set aside.

In a large, heavy skillet, heat the olive oil over high heat. If needed, pat the kale dry. Add the kale and onion to the pan and sauté for 3 minutes, stirring constantly. Add the garlic and sauté until the kale begins to wilt, about 2 minutes longer. Add the diluted vinegar. Remove the skillet from the heat and season with the red pepper flakes and salt to taste.

To serve, spread a portion of the turnip purée on each serving plate and place a few kale leaves on top. Spoon portions of the braised morel and sauteéd mushrooms on the kale and top with the pesto.

"It was so delicious. I love kale, and people rarely do it well."

NATALIE PORTMAN,
**ACTRESS AND
GUEST JUDGE**

ANDREW'S SQUASH SOUP

BOUQUET GARNI

1 bay leaf

4 to 6 sprigs fresh flat-leaf parsley

6 to 10 peppercorns

....

SQUASH SOUP

1 large butternut squash, halved and seeded

1 small acorn squash, halved and seeded

2 tablespoons olive oil

Salt and freshly ground pepper

Leaves from 1 bunch fresh sage

1/2 cup (1 stick) unsalted butter

3 leeks, white parts only, cleaned and sliced

2 carrots, peeled and sliced

3 shallots, sliced

1 clove garlic, minced

1/4 cup honey

1/4 cup white miso

6 cups vegetable stock or low-sodium broth

Cayenne pepper

....

VANILLA CRÈME FRAÎCHE

1 cup (8 ounces) crème fraîche

1 vanilla bean, split lengthwise

🕐 Prep time: 1 hour

🖵 Season 4, Episode 7

🔪 Elimination Challenge: Create a dish that combines a given color, emotion, and ingredient.

SERVES 6 TO 8

FOR THE BOUQUET GARNI: Wrap the bay leaf, parsley, and peppercorns in a square of cheesecloth or a coffee filter and tie securely with kitchen string.

FOR THE SQUASH SOUP: Preheat the oven to 350°F. Rub the cut sides of the squash halves with the olive oil and season with salt and pepper. Place the butternut squash halves, cut side down, on a baking sheet lined with parchment paper. Tuck several sage leaves under each squash half. Roast for about 10 minutes, then add the acorn squash, cut side down. Roast until squashes are tender when pierced with a knife, about 25 minutes longer. Remove from the oven and let cool for at least 10 minutes. Scoop the flesh out of each squash half and pass the flesh through a potato ricer or food mill. Set aside.

In a large, heavy-bottomed stockpot, melt the butter over medium heat. Add the leeks, carrots, shallots, and garlic and sweat until tender, about 10 minutes. Stir in the honey, scraping up any browned bits from the bottom of the pot. Stir in the miso until the vegetables are evenly coated. Add the puréed squash and the vegetable stock to the vegetable mixture. Cook over medium heat, stirring occasionally, until the mixture comes to a simmer, 15 to 20 minutes. Season with salt and cayenne pepper to taste. Keep the soup warm over low heat.

FOR THE VANILLA CRÈME FRAÎCHE: In a large bowl, whip the crème fraîche with a whisk until fluffy. Scrape the seeds from the vanilla bean with the tip of a paring knife and gently fold the seeds into the crème fraîche.

To serve, ladle the soup into warmed bowls and garnish each serving with a dollop of the vanilla crème fraîche.

ELI'S CLAM CHOWDER

CHOWDER

1 tablespoon unsalted butter

1 leek, white part only, halved lengthwise, cleaned and sliced

1 large russet potato, peeled and cut into large dice

1 clove garlic, minced

2 cups chicken stock or low-sodium broth

1/2 cup heavy cream

About 1 cup clam juice

Salt and freshly ground pepper

White truffle oil

....

CLAMS AND POTATOES

1/2 cup water

12 clams, preferably Manila or littleneck, scrubbed clean

1/2 russet potato, peeled and cut into large dice

Extra-virgin olive oil

Fresh lemon juice

4 fresh chives, minced

FENNEL SALAD

1 medium fennel bulb, trimmed (fronds reserved) and cut into brunoise

2 ribs celery, cut into brunoise, plus leaves, cut into chiffonade

1/2 cup fresh cilantro leaves, cut into chiffonade

White truffle oil

Fresh lemon juice

....

Crumbled crisply cooked bacon for garnish

SERVES 2

FOR THE CHOWDER: In a medium, heavy-bottomed stockpot, melt the butter over medium heat. Add the leek, potato, and garlic and sweat the mixture until the leek is translucent, about 5 minutes. Pour in the chicken stock, reduce the heat, and simmer until the potato is very tender, about 15 minutes. Transfer the mixture to a food processor or blender and process until smooth. Add the cream, then strain the soup through a fine-mesh sieve into a clean saucepan. Season to taste with the clam juice, salt and pepper, and truffle oil, and keep warm over low heat.

FOR THE CLAMS AND POTATOES: Bring the water to a boil in a small saucepan over high heat. Add the clams, reduce heat to medium, cover, and cook just until they open, 5 to 7 minutes. Discard any unopened clams. Remove the clams from their shells and put in a bowl.

Bring a small saucepan of water to a boil and have a bowl of ice water ready. Add the potato to the boiling water and cook until al dente, 5 to 7 minutes. Drain, shock in the ice bath, and drain again. Add the cooked potato to the clams and drizzle with olive oil and lemon juice to taste. Add the chives and toss.

FOR THE SALAD: In a medium bowl, combine the fennel, celery, celery leaves, and cilantro. Dress with white truffle oil and lemon juice to taste.

To serve, divide the potatoes and clams between 2 warmed bowls. Arrange the salad on top, dividing it in half. Pour chowder around the salad, and garnish with the bacon and reserved fennel fronds.

🕐 **Prep time:** 1½ hours

📺 **Season 6, Episode 8**

🔥 **Quickfire Challenge:**
Create a dish that pairs with a crunchy snack.

FABIO'S PASTA DEMO

Fabio Viviani, with his fabulous Florentine accent and fast moves, may not have won the title of Top Chef in Season 5, but he beat out charismatic Carla to capture the mantle of Fan Favorite. Perhaps his finest moment was winning the Last Supper Challenge by cooking roast chicken while nursing a broken hand.

"Who needs to throw sauce and garnish on top of his dish? It's like women with tons of makeup: once you take off the makeup you won't be happy with the result."

BIGGEST INFLUENCE: Grandma, because she cooked for ten hours a day for everyone and didn't wear makeup.

ADVICE FOR AMERICANS: Get rid of microwaves and boxed food.

LAST MEAL: Steak and pasta, and a bottle of wine. If I have to die after dinner, I want to be a little drunk.

ON FAN FAVORITE: I voted twenty times for Carla. She is hilarious and a great chef, and she deserved to win Fan Favorite as much as I did.

FABIO'S PASTA DOUGH

Fabio showed off his pasta-rolling chops a few times during the season. Here he shares how to make his perfect homemade ravioli.

1. Mound 5½ cups all-purpose flour on a clean work surface. Make a well in the center.

2. Add 2 tablespoons olive oil, 2 tablespoons water, a pinch of salt, and 8 egg yolks whisked with 2 whole eggs to the well. With a fork, begin to slowly work the flour into the egg mixture, cupping the outside of the wall of flour with your other hand to prevent the well from collapsing.

3. As the dough forms, use your hands to knead in all of the flour, forming a smooth ball. Cover the dough ball and let rest in the refrigerator for 1 hour.

4. Divide the dough into 4 pieces. Working with 1 piece at a time (and keeping the other pieces covered with a damp kitchen towel), roll the dough out with a rolling pin on a floured work surface into a strip 4 inches wide and ⅛ inch thick.

5. Alternatively, use a pasta machine. Flatten a dough piece into a rough rectangle about ½ inch thick and feed it through the widest setting on the machine 2 or 3 times. Dust the dough with flour if it starts to stick. Fold the dough into thirds, like folding a letter, turn the dial to the next narrower setting, and feed the dough through again, flouring as needed.

6. Repeat the folding and feeding process, working the dough from the widest to the narrowest setting until it is about ⅛ inch thick. Dust the work surface with flour and lay out the thin sheet of pasta to dry for at least 10 minutes. Repeat with the remaining 3 dough pieces. The dough is now ready to fill. For a filling idea, see Fabio's Mascarpone and Cashel Blue Ravioli (page 32).

Fabio's Favorite Ways to Serve Ravioli

- Plain, with Parmigiano-Reggiano and cracked black pepper

- With brown butter and sage

- With heirloom cherry tomato sauce and basil

- With melted Taleggio cheese and aged balsamic vinegar

- Serve them buck naked while singing Christmas carols—at that point the sauce really doesn't matter.

FABIO'S MASCARPONE AND CASHEL BLUE RAVIOLI

RAVIOLI FILLING

2 russet potatoes, peeled and quartered

1 cup (8 ounces) mascarpone cheese

5 ounces crumbled Cashel blue cheese

Salt and freshly ground pepper

PASTA

1 recipe Fabio's Pasta Dough (page 30)

1 egg

1 tablespoon water

Semolina flour or cornmeal for dusting

SAUCE

1 tablespoon olive oil

3 cloves garlic, minced

8 ounces white button mushrooms, brushed clean and chopped

Salt and freshly ground pepper

1 cup dry red wine

3/4 cup demi-glace

1 cup water

🕐 **Prep time:** 2 hours

🖥 Season 5, Episode 7

🔪 **Elimination Challenge:** Cook a dish that expresses your individuality.

PASTA RATIO

1 cup flour: 1 egg

Pasta dough can be made from this very simple ratio. In Fabio's technique, you combine whole eggs with separated egg yolks and a bit of water for a richer and more pliable dough. Chef Mark Peel uses a similar ratio but with duck eggs for his fettuccine (facing page).

SERVES 8 TO 10

FOR THE RAVIOLI FILLING: In a saucepan, boil the potatoes in salted water to cover until tender, about 15 minutes. Drain, transfer to a food processor, add both cheeses, and pulse until smooth. Season with salt and pepper.

FOR THE PASTA: Roll out the pasta dough as instructed. Trim each sheet so it is about 4 inches wide. Cover with plastic wrap.

In a small bowl, beat the egg with the water. Uncover 1 pasta sheet and brush with the egg wash. Drop tablespoonfuls of the potato-cheese filling lengthwise along half of the sheet, spacing them about 2 inches apart. Fold over the other half of the pasta sheet to cover the filling, then gently press around each mound of filling to eliminate any air pockets. With a knife, cut out the ravioli squares, then crimp the edges with the tines of a fork to seal the ravioli closed. Place the ravioli on a baking sheet sprinkled with semolina flour. Set aside. Repeat with the remaining pasta sheets.

FOR THE SAUCE: Heat the olive oil in a medium saucepan over medium-high heat. Add the garlic and mushrooms and sauté until the mushrooms are browned and tender, 10 to 15 minutes. Season with salt and pepper. Add the wine and stir to scrape up any browned bits from the bottom of the pan. Cook until the wine is nearly absorbed, about 10 minutes. Add the demi-glace and water and simmer until the sauce is thick enough to coat a spoon. Transfer the sauce to a blender and purée. Strain through a fine-mesh sieve into a clean saucepan. Set aside.

To serve, bring a large pot of salted water to a boil. Add the ravioli and cook until just tender, 2 to 3 minutes. Divide among dinner plates and top with the sauce.

MARK PEEL'S DUCK-EGG PASTA CARBONARA

CREAM SAUCE

2 cups heavy cream

2 slices applewood–smoked bacon, cut into large dice

4 egg yolks

3 tablespoons buttermilk

2 tablespoons finely chopped fresh tarragon

1/2 cup extra-virgin olive oil

DUCK-EGG PASTA

2 cups all-purpose flour

1 teaspoon kosher salt

4 duck-egg yolks

1/4 cup cold water

3 tablespoons extra-virgin olive oil

SERVES 4

FOR THE CREAM SAUCE: In a medium saucepan over medium-high heat, combine the cream and bacon and bring to a simmer. Cook until the cream is reduced by one-third, about 15 minutes. Remove from the heat and let cool to room temperature. Strain into a medium bowl and whisk in the egg yolks, buttermilk, and tarragon. Slowly stream in the olive oil while continuously whisking, until the cream mixture thickens.

FOR THE DUCK-EGG PASTA: On a clean work surface, mound the flour and use your fingers to form a well in the center of the mound. Put the salt, egg yolks, water, and olive oil in the well. With a fork, begin to slowly work the flour into the egg mixture, cupping the outside of the wall of flour with your other hand to prevent the well from collapsing. Once a dough forms, use your hands to knead in all of the flour, forming a smooth, elastic ball. Wrap the dough ball in plastic wrap and let rest in the refrigerator for 30 minutes.

Roll out the dough as instructed on page 30. Cut each pasta sheet into sections about 4 inches wide and 10 inches long.

Cut the pasta sheets lengthwise into 1/2-inch-wide strips with a knife, or use the cutting attachment on the pasta machine to cut fettuccine.

To serve, bring a large pot of salted water to a boil. Add the pasta and cook until just tender but still al dente, 2 to 3 minutes. Drain. Toss the pasta with the cream sauce and divide among 4 plates.

Prep time: 1 hour

Top Chef Masters, Season 1, Episode 4

Elimination Challenge: Make an egg dish while using only one hand.

Q+A

WITH
nikki

This strong-minded native New Yorker had worked with some of the biggest chefs in the land before finding acclaim as chef and partner of 24 Prince in New York City. On the show, Nikki Cascone was pegged as the pasta and Italian food chef of Season 4. She was sent home for her lack of team leadership in the Wedding Wars competition and is now planning to open a second restaurant.

How would you describe your signature style of cooking/philosophy of food?

I don't think it's pretty unique, it's actually a big trend right now, but it's organic and seasonal. Very much farm to table. That's my style.

How did you feel about being the pasta queen of *Top Chef*?

I hated it. For a long time I had people come into 24 Prince and be surprised that it wasn't an Italian restaurant. They get mad that there was no fresh pasta on the menu. You have to deal with the editing of the show and being pegged a certain way. It was hard at first; I was resentful because I felt like that was all I was being remembered for. But now I'm embracing it and starting a pasta bar.

What are your favorite pastas?

Baked pasta (I love getting the cheesiness and the crunch), ravioli (or any kind of stuffed pasta), any kind of buckwheat pasta, and all the classics (ziti, lasagna, spaghetti and meatballs).

What are your favorite sauces?

I'm a pretty simple gal. I like olive oil with roasted pepper flakes and roasted garlic. I'll add escarole, roasted tomato, fresh basil, and pecorino to a pasta dish.

What are the most common mistake people make when making pasta?

Over-working the dough, adding too much flour. You really have to learn—like any good bread maker—how to work with the dough. That is the part that's an art. You have to become Zen with the dough.

Are there any places you've traveled that have inspired your cooking style?

Just about everywhere you go, as a chef, inspires you. I went to a food and wine festival in Jamaica, and I really got inspired by their jerk flavors. I am very inspired by the Mediterranean. I haven't been to any of the Asian countries yet, but being on the show with a lot of Asian influenced chefs, I came home and started experimenting with Asian flavors.

What advice can you give beginning chefs?

Eliminate fear from cooking and open your mind. There is such an amazing large vast world of food, and if you are afraid, you are not going to experience it. Build a library of ingredients so that you can teach yourself how to use those ingredients in a lot of different ways. If you know how to use an ingredient you will know it forever.

TOP TEAM

Every season, groups of chef'testants bond together in different ways. What was your favorite team to root for?

TEAM RAINBOW

Richard S., Jamie, and Patrick formed the gay chef rainbow coalition on Season 5, only to see its sudden disbanding after Patrick was eliminated at the end of the first episode.

TEAM EURO

Fabio and Stefan stole the show on Season 5. With strong accents and strong personalities —one prickly, the other charming—it was Eurolove at first sight.

TEAM VOLTAGGIO

Michael and Bryan's ultracompetitive, love-hate relationship kept things interesting on Season 6. Get the dish from the brothers themselves on page 62.

ASHLEY'S TRUFFLED GNOCCHI

4 russet potatoes, scrubbed

1 cup arugula leaves, blanched and shocked (see page 15), then drained

1/2 cup heavy cream

2 tablespoons unsalted butter, melted, plus 2 tablespoons at room temperature

Salt and freshly ground pepper

All-purpose flour for dusting

4 egg yolks

Freshly grated nutmeg

1 tablespoon olive oil

1 shallot, minced

1 clove garlic, sliced into thin rounds

2 cups hen of the woods (*maitake*) mushrooms, brushed clean and broken apart

Leaves from 2 sprigs fresh thyme, chopped

Ricotta cheese for garnish

Finely chopped fresh chives for garnish

White truffle oil for drizzling

SERVES 8

Preheat the oven to 350°F. Pierce the potatoes with a fork in several places and bake until tender, about 45 minutes. Remove from the oven and let cool until warm. Meanwhile, combine the arugula, cream, and melted butter in a small bowl. Season to taste with salt and pepper and set aside.

Scoop the potato flesh from the skins and pass through a food mill or ricer onto a clean work surface dusted with flour. You should have about 4 cups. Gather the potato into a mound and make a well in the center. Put the egg yolks in the well. Grate in a touch of nutmeg and add a pinch of salt. Using two bench scrapers or a fork, mix the dough together with a chopping motion. Roll the dough into a large log. Working in batches, pull off a small amount of dough and gently knead it on the floured surface until shiny. Roll into a long rope about 1/2 inch in diameter. Dust with flour and set aside. Repeat with the remaining dough.

Bring a large pot of salted water to a boil. Cut the ropes into chunks of dough about the length of your finger from tip to first joint.

In a large sauté pan, warm the olive oil over medium heat. Add the shallot and sauté until soft, about 5 minutes. Add the garlic, mushrooms, and thyme and cook until the mushrooms are lightly browned and soft, about 5 minutes. Keep warm over low heat.

Add the gnocchi to the boiling water, cooking in batches as needed to avoid crowding. When the gnocchi float, after about 1 minute, remove them from the water with a slotted spoon and add them to pan with the mushrooms. Add the room-temperature butter and stir to coat.

To serve, spoon a portion of the arugula-cream sauce onto each plate. Arrange the gnocchi and mushrooms on top. Garnish with the ricotta and fresh chives. Drizzle lightly with the truffle oil.

Prep time: 2 hours

Season 6, Episode 3

Quickfire Challenge: Create a dish from an assortment of potatoes.

HUBERT KELLER'S MAC AND CHEESE

Unsalted butter for greasing, plus 4 tablespoons

1 pound elbow macaroni

1 pound small to medium shrimp, peeled and deveined

3 large carrots, peeled and cut into medium dice

1 large onion, cut into medium dice

1 cup thinly sliced white mushrooms

3 cups heavy cream

1/2 cup half-and-half

Salt and freshly ground pepper

1 1/2 cups shredded Swiss cheese

6 egg yolks, beaten

5 tablespoons finely chopped fresh flat-leaf parsley

SERVES 6 TO 8

Preheat the oven to 400°F. Butter a 9-by-13-inch baking dish.

Bring a large pot of salted water to a boil over high heat. Add the macaroni and cook until al dente, about 8 minutes. Drain, rinse with cold water, and set aside.

Bring a medium pot of water to boil over high heat. Add the shrimp and cook until opaque throughout, about 3 minutes. Drain and set aside.

In a large saucepan over medium-high heat, combine the 4 tablespoons butter, carrots, onion, and mushrooms and sweat until tender, about 10 minutes. Add 2 cups of the cream, the half-and-half, and salt and pepper to taste. Reduce the heat and simmer until the mixture thickens, 10 to 15 minutes. Remove from heat and stir in the cheese until creamy. Add the shrimp and pasta and mix gently until well combined. Spread the mixture in the prepared dish.

In a bowl, using an electric mixer, beat the remaining 1 cup cream to soft peaks. Gently fold the egg yolks and parsley into the whipped cream. Pour this mixture over the macaroni mixture.

Bake until bubbly and golden, about 30 minutes.

To serve, divide among 6 to 8 dinner plates.

Prep time: 1 hour, 30 minutes

Top Chef Masters, Season 1, Episode 1

Elimination Challenge: Create a meal using only a dorm-room microwave, toaster oven, and hot plate.

HUBERT KELLER DISHES

"This was one of those moments when you are really put in a corner, and you just have to figure something out. I was cooking pasta and there was no sink; I was caught by surprise. I thought to myself, I will not be kicked off because of a pasta! So I went into the shower to drain the pasta, stop the cooking by rinsing it with cold water, and warm my plates with the steam. That has become a classic moment, much like the finger-in-the-sauce incident at Fleur de Lys from the very first Quickfire Challenge."

Q+A

michael chiarello

Maestro of rustic Italian cooking, TV regular, and chef-owner of Bottega in Napa Valley, Michael Chiarello nearly walked away with the title of Top Chef Master. Despite being away from the stoves for several years, Michael proved he could go head-to-head with the best of them as he battled through challenges, including making Quinoa Pasta (page 43) taste good. For his beautifully narrative finale dinner, he concocted polenta so creamy the judges wanted to "bathe in it" and a slow-braised short-rib dish that had the diners sighing wistfully into their plates. He also starred as a guest judge in the Season 6 finale.

What was it like competing on *Top Chef Masters*?
The experience was fantastic. It was a great test of yourself. It's like a ropes course. You put the right cast of characters together and you know you're going to get a good show. And that's what happened.

Do you think your extensive TV experience gave you an edge?
I knew how much faster time goes on TV, so I was prepared for the time constraints. Also, after doing my own show for so many years, I'm used to working alone without sous-chefs.

What was it like working alongside the other Masters?
It was awesome. Most of us are friends; we've met before and done a lot of benefits together. The most fun we had was in the green room, talking about food and drinking wine.

Which challenge on the show did you especially enjoy?
The finale was by far my favorite because we got a chance to tell a story, and I'm a storyteller. We always talk about the difference between taste and flavor. I can just put a short rib down on your table, or I can tell you that I smoked it in Cabernet vines that come from my vineyard and that it was inspired by the dead of winter when the wood fire is going. That's exciting to me as a storyteller, with my medium being food. We finally felt like they had taken off our handcuffs when we did that challenge.

What was it like facing a panel of critics?
Standing up there was difficult because it's not just me I'm representing—it's my family, my crew at the restaurant. You're trying not to let everyone down. It's one thing to get a smack; it's another thing to get a smack in front of millions of viewers. All you can do is listen to the critics, and see if you agree. You're probably standing there for two hours. It's like a firing squad.

How would you describe your style of cooking?
Extremely ingredient driven. I try to put the technique behind the ingredients, not in front of them. I try to take food and present it in a new way that people would never have imagined.

Who has inspired your cooking the most?
My family background probably has been the greatest influence. We grew up in this very Calabrese fashion: drying tomatoes, picking wild fennel, making our own prosciutto and salami. I continue those traditions at the restaurant.

Do you get a lot of inspiration from Napa Valley?
I get a tremendous amount of inspiration from Napa Valley. Right now we are just starting to sort the Zinfandel grapes at my vineyard. We'll make preserved jelly to serve for the cheese course. We'll take the leaves and cook them.

What's hot in Italian cuisine right now?
I see food getting more regionally specific, and I think that's an exciting trend. I think the new pizza trend is awesome. The old is new again. Cooking things that are more authentic is actually very progressive.

What's your quick comfort food?
I like pasta with toasted bread crumbs, aged pecorino, fresh mint, and dried Calabrian chile. I think sauce shouldn't take longer than the time it takes to cook the pasta.

What are some of your favorite ingredients?
- Gray salt from Brittany, the salt we use exclusively.
- Olive oil. We use a half dozen different ones.
- *Mosto cotto* (cooked grape juice).
- Polenta. I get a special kind that comes from outside Venice.
- All the cured meats that we make.
- Pasta: just flour, salt, water, and egg.
- Eggs are one of my favorite ingredients.

MICHAEL CHIARELLO'S QUINOA PASTA

SALSA VERDE

Leaves from 2 bunches fresh flat-leaf parsley

Leaves from 1 bunch fresh basil

12 cornichons, coarsely chopped

2 tablespoons capers, rinsed

4 cloves garlic, coarsely chopped

1 cup extra-virgin olive oil, or as needed

Sea salt and freshly ground pepper

PINE NUT *GREMOLATA*

1/2 cup gluten-free crackers

1/4 cup pine nuts

1/4 cup fresh flat-leaf parsley leaves

1 tablespoon grated lemon zest

1 tablespoon minced garlic

Sea salt and freshly ground pepper

PASTA

1 pound quinoa spaghetti

2 tablespoons olive oil

6 cloves garlic, sliced

1 tablespoon capers, rinsed

1/4 teaspoon red pepper flakes

6 zucchini, cut lengthwise into thin slices

....

2 cups Oven-Dried Tomatoes (below)

SERVES 4

FOR THE SALSA VERDE: Bring a pot of water to a boil. Blanch and shock the parsley and basil (see page 15). When cool, drain, squeeze out the excess water, and chop coarsely. In a food processor or blender, combine the herbs with the cornichons, capers, garlic, and olive oil and process until well combined. Season with salt and pepper and adjust the consistency with more olive oil, if needed. Set aside.

FOR THE PINE NUT *GREMOLATA*: In a food processor, combine the crackers, pine nuts, and parsley and process until finely chopped. Pulse in the lemon zest and garlic, and season to taste with salt and pepper. Set aside.

FOR THE PASTA: Bring a large pot of salted water to a boil. Add the pasta and cook until al dente, about 8 minutes.

Meanwhile, in a large sauté pan, heat the olive oil over medium heat. Add the garlic and sauté for 1 minute. Stir in the capers and red pepper flakes. Add 1 cup of the pasta water and the zucchini to the pan and bring to a simmer while the pasta finishes.

Drain the pasta. Add the pasta and salsa verde to the pan with the zucchini. With the pan still over heat, toss to combine.

To serve, spoon the oven-dried tomatoes around the circumference of each serving plate. Using tongs, arrange a nest of the pasta in the center of the plate and top with the *gremolata*.

Prep time: 45 minutes

Top Chef Masters, Season 1, Episode 8

Elimination Challenge: Create a vegan dish without gluten or soy.

HOW TO MAKE

oven-dried tomatoes

2 pints cherry tomatoes, halved

1/2 cup garlic cloves, cut into thin slices

1/4 cup balsamic vinegar

1 cup fresh basil leaves

2 teaspoons sea salt

Pinch of red pepper flakes

Preheat the oven to 275°F. Put the tomatoes and garlic on a baking sheet. Sprinkle with the vinegar, basil, salt, and red pepper flakes and toss to combine well. Spread in an even layer. Bake until the tomatoes are soft and darkened, about 2 hours.

EGGS SIX WAYS

Although it seems simple, cooking an egg can be a telling gauge of a chef's ability. It takes sensitivity and experience to know just when to take it off the heat, when the white is no longer a slimy fright but before it turns into latex. As we've seen in the various breakfast challenges, the beauty of eggs is how versatile they can be, from casual breakfast to elegant entrée.

SCRAMBLED: You might not serve your scrambled eggs in a cut-off eggshell with one hand tied behind your back like Anita Lo did on *Top Chef Masters* (page 133), but proper technique still applies. Whisk together eggs, a bit of cream, and a pinch of salt in a bowl before pouring them into a nonstick pan. Cook them gently over low heat, and serve immediately.

FRIED: Fried eggs are nothing if not versatile. In Season 5, Leah showed off her finesse with a mini breakfast sandwich using a tiny quail egg. In a later episode, during the TV Demo Quickfire Challenge, Jamie was frustrated by a fried duck egg whose yolk had not set. When frying an egg, add a little water to the pan and cover it if you want a firmer yolk.

OVER EASY: A variation of the fried theme, "over easy" simply means a fried egg that is flipped in order to firm up the yolk before serving, hopefully without breaking it. In the Padma breakfast challenge in Season 6, Eli made his eggs over easy in the winning Huevos Cubanos dish (page 130).

POACHED: On the sophisticated end of egg prep, poaching takes practice and patience. Antonia used poached eggs beautifully in several salads during Season 4, and even earned accolades on the egg line at Lou Mitchell's in Chicago. Use poached eggs as part of a lunch or brunch on a salad of frisée with bacon, or on an English muffin with ham and hollandaise to make eggs Benedict.

BAKED: On *Top Chef Masters,* John Besh was overconfident about his baked eggs, which probably would have been delicious if they had finished in time. To bake eggs at home, preheat the oven to 375°F and butter individual ramekins or small gratins. Break 1 or 2 eggs directly into each ramekin and bake until the eggs are set but not hard, 10 to 15 minutes.

SLOW-COOKED: On *Top Chef Masters*, Wylie Dufresne used an immersion circulator to make slow-cooked eggs, and Richard B. used a similar technique in the Season 5 finale. To replicate these methods, place your eggs in a pot filled with cold water and slowly heat the water until it reaches 150°F (you will need to use a deep-frying or candy thermometer). Gently cook for 30 minutes, rotating the eggs occasionally to center the yolk.

TOP CHEF PERSONALS

Sure, most of these Season 6 chefs are in committed relationships, but we still wanted to find out what it takes to be compatible with these culinary cuties. Would you rather eat your way around the world with Michael V. or enjoy a romantic rib eye for two with Ashley? What's your ideal first date: Thai food with Eli or a few rounds of bourbon with Kevin?

Michael Voltaggio (a.k.a. Squigs)

Passionate, soulful, ambitious. Christian faith. Loves In-N-Out burgers, Ben & Jerry's ice cream, gin and tonics. Wants to eat in as many three-star Michelin restaurants as possible. Idea of a romantic night in involves making a pizza together at home.

Ashley Merriman (a.k.a. The Ace)

Intuitive, tender, charismatic. Former sex ed teacher. Loves a good margarita: Cointreau, tequila, salt, ice. Lifelong ambition: to own a farm. Wine and dine with foie gras *torchon*, scallops, and a bone-in rib eye for two, with an outstanding bottle of red.

Bryan Voltaggio (a.k.a. Volty)

Passionate, driven, optimistic. Enjoys traveling—next up: India, Spain, Tokyo, Istanbul. Weakness for popcorn. Obsessed with the color navy blue, has owned four navy blue Jeeps. Would like to be Jack Bauer in next life.

Eli Kirshtein

Funny, caring, eccentric. Huge jokester and home comedian. Slightly lactose intolerant. Enjoys cheese biscuits, despite lactose intolerance. Perfect first-date food is Asian, like Thai, to show a little flair. Great Italian food and dim lights make for a romantic evening.

Kevin Gillespie (a.k.a. Bubba)

Reliable, witty, full of conviction. Once with two friends ate four hundred hot wings in one hour. Drinks an old-fashioned or bourbon neat. First kiss at nine years old on Valentine's Day. Would like to one day work at Michel Bras.

Mike Isabella (a.k.a. Izzy)

Driven, passionate, fun. Dreams of traveling the world and one day becoming a black belt in mixed martial arts. Sucker for Reese's Peanut Butter Cups and Ketel One and tonic. Also goes by Jersey or Bella.

Robin Leventhal (a.k.a. Salt Lick)

Optimistic, nurturing, passionate. Earthy girl who loves natural sciences. Cancer survivor. Enjoys Junior Mints, CornNuts, and the color periwinkle. First kiss was at camp, when eight or nine, in a bunk-bed tent. Would like to make Padma drool.

Laurine Wickett (a.k.a. Sunshine)

Confident, sassy, focused. Sci-fi geek into *Star Wars* and *Lord of the Rings*. Used to sell grilled cheese sandwiches for a buck on the lots of Grateful Dead shows. Likes a cheap first date, pizza and beer—doesn't cost a lot if it doesn't work out.

45

PRINCIPLES OF PROTEIN:
BEEF, LAMB, PORK, POULTRY

73

65

55

69

75

HOW TO COOK MEAT

Juicy grilled pork chops. A perfectly roasted chicken. The caramelized exterior of a pan-seared steak. Meat is the cornerstone of so many great meals, and cooking it properly is part of the foundation of any chef's skills.

ROASTING

The perfect method for large-yet-tender cuts, such as a rack of lamb, standing rib roast, or bone-in pork loin. Use a heavy roasting pan and just enough oil that the meat doesn't stick.

PAN-ROASTING

Great for cooking steaks and chops of all kinds. A heavy-duty stainless-steel sauté pan or cast-iron skillet over medium-high heat works great. Start with a little olive oil, and when the meat is cooked, you can use the pan to create a flavorful sauce. For very thick steaks, you can put the pan in a hot oven to finish the cooking.

GRILLING AND BROILING

Meat cooked on a charcoal or gas grill yields quick and delicious results. Use a marinade or rub to add flavor to flank or skirt steak. A porterhouse or New York strip simply seasoned with salt and pepper and grilled to medium-rare makes a wonderful main dish. Broiling is similar to grilling, using high heat at close range. Slather your steak or chop with mustard, slide it under the broiler for a few minutes, and you've got dinner.

STEWING AND BRAISING

The key ingredient in these moist-heat techniques is time. Don't rush the braise or let the cooking liquid boil, and your brisket, veal shank, or short ribs will be meltingly tender, never tough. Michael Chiarello braised his short ribs so expertly that he nearly walked away with the title of Top Chef Master.

WHEN IS IT DONE?

If *Top Chef* has taught us one thing, it's don't undercook or overcook your proteins. In Season 6, Hector was sent home for the uneven cooking of his chateaubriand in the French Classics Elimination, and in Season 3, Sara M. was sent packing right before the finale for her "pink" chicken. Often restaurant cooks are so attuned to cooking meat that they can tell when it's ready just by looking and listening. Here are some tips for the rest of us.

THE THERMOMETER TEST: A meat thermometer is the most efficient tool for helping you know when meat is done. Make sure to take the meat off the heat shortly *before* it reaches the desired temperature, and let it rest, loosely tented in aluminum foil, for 5 to 10 minutes. The meat will continue to cook a little more as it rests.

THE TOUCH TEST: Try to catch the meat at the moment it has just the right amount of give when you press on it. If it still feels very loose and jiggly when you touch it, it's not done. If it feels hard and immovable, you've overcooked it.

THE KNIFE TEST: When in doubt, cut into it and take a peek. This is the surefire way to know if it is still raw in the middle.

seared

rare

medium-rare

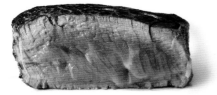

medium

medium-well

well-done

ASHLEY'S FOIE GRAS WITH PINEAPPLE

1 tablespoon unsalted butter

½ fresh pineapple, cut into ¼-inch-thick slices

Leaves from 1 bunch fresh tarragon some reserved for garnish

1 cup extra-virgin olive oil

4 ounces fresh foie gras, cut into 4 bite-sized slices

Salt and freshly ground pepper

🕐 **Prep time:** 20 minutes

📺 **Season 6, Episode 4**

🔥 **Quickfire Challenge:** Compete in a 20-minute *amuse-bouche* cook-off.

ASHLEY DISHES

"Talk about pressure—one bite of food and I could have been done! When I got into the kitchen, the entire place was a disaster. It was as if a herd of elephants had come through and turned the place upside down. I did find some lukewarm foie gras, which I packed in ice to try and cool it down, so I could cut it nicely and get a good sear on it. I love pairing acidic fruit with foie gras; it cuts through the fattiness of the foie."

SERVES 4

Heat a large sauté pan over high heat. Melt the butter and add the pineapple. Cook, turning once, until the pineapple is crisp-tender and caramelized, about 5 minutes. Let cool, then dice. Set aside.

Bring a saucepan of water to a boil. Blanch and shock the tarragon (see page 15), then drain. In a blender, purée the tarragon with the olive oil.

In a medium sauté pan, warm 2 tablespoons of the tarragon oil over medium-high heat. Season the foie gras with salt and pepper. Add to the hot pan and sear, turning once, about 2 minutes per side.

To serve, mound some pineapple on each of 4 plates. Top with a piece of foie gras and garnish with fresh tarragon leaves. Drizzle the plate with tarragon oil. (The remaining tarragon oil will keep in an airtight container in the refrigerator for up to 1 week.)

"This Quickfire challenged the chef'testants' ability to quickly come up with a dish that showcased their talents. Reaching deep into your repertoire is the best move you can make in such a situation."

BRYAN, SEASON 6

TOP MEAT

Over the years, we've seen chef'testants butcher whole hogs, break down little lambs, and even wrestle with creatures like alligators and snakes.

King of Speed:
Season 3, Episode 10
Hung made *Top Chef* history when he chopped up four whole chickens in record time in this Mise-en-Place Relay.

Going Whole Hog:
Season 4, Episode 13
The four finalists (Stephanie, Richard B., Lisa, and Antonia) had to cook an entire pig in Puerto Rico.

Toaster-Oven Turkey:
Season 5, Episode 3
Chef'testants had to cook a Thanksgiving dinner using only microwaves and large-size toaster ovens. Ariane turned out a succulent turkey breast (see page 55).

Chicken Chase:
Season 5, Episode 8
Team Chicken (Stefan, Jamie, and Carla) chased live chickens around the coop for this challenge on the farm.

Show Your Chops:
Season 4, Episode 12
Spike won this challenge by expertly frenching a rack of tomahawk chops at a meatpacking facility. He also cooked up a mean tomahawk chop (see page 75).

Porkopolis:
Season 6, Episode 8
Claiming a close personal relationship with pork, Kevin snatched the title at the Pigs and Pinot Elimination with his Pork Terrine with Pickled Cherries (page 159).

FABIO'S ROASTED CHICKEN AND POTATOES

ROASTED CHICKEN

1 whole roasting chicken, 6 to 7 pounds

¼ cup finely chopped fresh rosemary, plus 4 sprigs

1 bunch fresh sage

Kosher salt and freshly ground pepper

6 cloves garlic

1 lemon, halved lengthwise

ROASTED POTATOES

Olive oil for greasing

6 russet potatoes, peeled and cut into large dice

10 cloves garlic, smashed

2 tablespoons chopped fresh rosemary

Salt and freshly ground pepper

CARAMELIZED ONIONS

2 pounds cipollini onions

2 tablespoons unsalted butter

Salt and freshly ground pepper

1 tablespoon balsamic vinegar

🕐 **Prep time:** 2 hours

🖥 Season 5, Episode 12

🔪 Elimination Challenge:
Create a five-course meal selected by one of five culinary luminaries.

ABOUT AN INGREDIENT

roasters

It's unlikely you'll find a real rooster for *coq au vin* at your local supermarket, but you will see fryers and roasters for sale, even in this age of prepackaged food. The main difference between a fryer and a roaster chicken is size. Fryers are younger and smaller, 2½ to 4 pounds. A roaster, on the other hand, usually weighs in at 4 to 7 pounds.

SERVES 4

FOR THE CHICKEN: Preheat the oven to 475°F.

Rinse the chicken under cold water and pat dry. Trim any excess fat. Loosen the skin from the breast and thighs with your fingers and spread the chopped rosemary, a few leaves of sage, and generous pinches of kosher salt beneath the skin. Stuff the rosemary sprigs and remaining sage sprigs and the garlic cloves into the cavity of the chicken.

In a dry skillet over high heat, grill the lemon halves, cut sides down, until browned, about 2 minutes, and add them to the cavity. Season the outside of the chicken with salt and pepper. Bring the wings up and over the back to tuck the tips under the chicken. Tie the legs together with kitchen string. Place the chicken in a roasting pan, breast side up, and roast for 10 minutes. Reduce the oven temperature to 375°F and continue to roast until a meat thermometer inserted in the thickest part of a thigh but not touching bone registers 170°F, 30 to 40 minutes longer. Remove the chicken from the oven, tent loosely with aluminum foil, and let rest for 10 minutes.

FOR THE POTATOES: Preheat the oven to 375°F. Oil a large roasting pan.

Bring a large pot of salted water to a boil. Add the potatoes and parboil until they are just soft enough to poke with a toothpick, about 5 minutes. Drain well. Put the potatoes in the prepared roasting pan and toss them with the garlic, rosemary, and salt and pepper to taste. Roast until crispy and golden, about 30 minutes.

FOR THE ONIONS: Bring a large pot of salted water to a boil. Add the onions and parboil for 5 minutes. Drain, let cool, and peel. Transfer the onions to a large, heavy skillet over medium heat. Add the butter and slowly cook the onions until they begin to caramelize, about 15 minutes. Season with salt and pepper and add the balsamic vinegar. Continue to cook over medium heat, stirring occasionally, until golden brown, about 25 minutes longer.

To serve, carve the chicken into slices of breast meat and serving-sized pieces of leg and thigh. Place a serving of potatoes on each plate and place the chicken on top of the potatoes, fanning out the breast meat slices. Add a portion of the onions on the side of each plate.

"The potatoes were killer. I challenge anyone to match the potatoes of my grandma."

FABIO, SEASON 5

ARIANE'S ORANGE-BRINED TURKEY BREAST

TURKEY

1½ cups water

1 cup fresh orange juice

2 tablespoons salt

1 tablespoon sugar

8 sprigs fresh thyme

2 tablespoons grated orange zest

1 tablespoon black peppercorns

1 whole turkey breast (not kosher), 5 to 6 pounds, deboned, breast-bones reserved

Olive oil for rubbing

Freshly ground pepper

....

TURKEY GRAVY

Reserved breast bones (above)

2 carrots, peeled and cut into rondelles

3 ribs celery, cut into large dice

2 bay leaves

1 tablespoon white peppercorns

8 cups chicken stock or low-sodium broth

¼ cup Wondra flour

3 tablespoons unsalted butter

3 shallots, minced

1 pound baby portobello mushrooms, brushed clean and sliced

SERVES 6

FOR THE TURKEY: In a saucepan, combine the water, orange juice, salt, sugar, thyme, orange zest, and peppercorns. Bring to a boil over high heat. Remove from the heat and let cool. Place the turkey in a nonreactive container, pour the brine over, cover, and refrigerate for at least 1 hour or up to 4 hours.

Preheat the oven to 350°F. Remove the turkey from the brine and pat dry with paper towels. Let stand at room temperature for at least 30 minutes or up to 2 hours.

Put the turkey in a heavy roasting pan. Rub with olive oil and season with pepper. Roast until the skin is golden brown and a meat thermometer inserted in the thickest part registers 155° to 160°F, about 1 hour. Let rest for 15 minutes.

FOR THE GRAVY: Chop the breast bones and put them in a stockpot. Add the carrots, celery, bay leaves, peppercorns, and stock and place over medium heat. Simmer gently for 1 hour, adjusting the heat as necessary. Strain through a fine-mesh sieve into a clean pot. Bring to a boil over medium-high heat and whisk in the flour. Reduce the heat to medium and cook until thickened to the desired gravylike consistency, 15 to 30 minutes. Set aside. Keep warm.

In a medium sauté pan, melt the butter over medium heat. Add the shallots and mushrooms and raise the heat to medium-high. Cook until the mushrooms brown, about 10 minutes. Season with salt and pepper and add to the gravy.

To serve, slice the turkey, arrange on plates, and ladle the gravy over the top.

Prep time: 2 hours, plus 1 to 4 hours for brining

Season 5, Episode 3

Elimination Challenge: Make Thanksgiving dinner for the rock band Foo Fighters.

STEFAN'S ROASTED DUCK WITH PRETZEL DUMPLINGS

CABBAGE

1 tablespoon vegetable oil

1 large onion, cut into thin slices

1 small red cabbage, cored and julienned

4 small apples, peeled, cored, and grated on the large holes of a box grater

1 cup lingonberry jam

1 cinnamon stick

1/4 teaspoon ground cloves

2 cups apple juice

2 cups port wine

2 cups dry red wine

2 bay leaves

1 teaspoon salt

2 tablespoons duck fat

Freshly ground pepper

PRETZEL DUMPLINGS

1 tablespoon vegetable oil

1 small onion, minced

2 cups milk

6 slices white bread, crusts removed and torn into large pieces

1 cup crumbled hard pretzels

1 cup mushrooms, preferably chanterelle, brushed clean and cut into medium dice

3 egg yolks, lightly beaten

1 whole egg, lightly beaten

Leaves from 2 sprigs fresh marjoram, minced

Salt and freshly ground pepper

4 tablespoons unsalted butter

2 tablespoons minced fresh flat-leaf parsley

Freshly grated nutmeg

DUCK BREASTS

2 boneless, skin-on whole duck breasts

Salt and freshly ground pepper

5 sprigs fresh rosemary

3 cloves garlic, sliced lengthwise

SERVES 4

FOR THE CABBAGE: In a heavy-bottomed pot, heat the oil over medium heat. Add the onion and sauté until translucent, about 5 minutes. Add the cabbage, apples, jam, cinnamon stick, cloves, apple juice, port, red wine, bay leaves, and salt and raise the heat to high. Bring to a boil, reduce the heat to low, and simmer until the cabbage is tender, about 2 hours. Remove and discard the cinnamon stick and bay leaves. Add the duck fat. Adjust the seasoning with pepper and additional salt, if necessary.

FOR THE PRETZEL DUMPLINGS: Bring a large pot of salted water to a boil. Meanwhile, in a sauté pan, heat the oil over medium-high heat. Add the onion and sauté until translucent and soft, about 4 minutes. Add the milk and bring to a boil. Remove from the heat and let cool for 2 or 3 minutes.

Meanwhile, pulse the bread and pretzels in a food processor to break into 1/4-inch pieces. Transfer to a large bowl and stir in the mushrooms, egg yolks, whole egg, and marjoram. Season with salt and pepper. Pour the heated milk and onions into the bowl and toss the ingredients with a fork until evenly moistened and well combined.

CONTINUED

Prep time: 2 hours

Season 5, Episode 7

Elimination Challenge:
Cook a dish that expresses your individuality.

Working in batches as needed to avoid crowding, drop heaping tablespoonfuls (alternatively, shape between your palms into balls about 1 inch in diameter) of the dough into the boiling water and cook until the dumplings float to the surface, about 2 minutes. With a slotted spoon, remove the dumplings from the water and set aside on a plate.

FOR THE DUCK BREAST: Preheat the oven to 400°F.

Score the skin of the duck breasts in a crosshatch pattern with a sharp knife, taking care not to cut into the meat below the fat. Season the breasts with salt and pepper. Heat a large, ovenproof skillet over medium-high heat. Lay the rosemary and garlic in the pan and put the duck breasts on top, skin side down. Sear until the fat is well rendered and the skin is golden brown and crisp, about 8 minutes. Remove the skillet from the heat, remove the garlic and the rosemary sprigs, and drain off the fat (use to flavor the cabbage). Turn the duck breasts skin side up and transfer the skillet to the oven to finish cooking to the desired doneness, about 3 minutes for medium-rare (135°F). Remove the duck breasts from the oven and set them aside to rest for 5 minutes.

To serve, melt the butter in a medium sauté pan over medium-high heat. Stir in the parsley and nutmeg to taste, then add the dumplings and sauté until slightly golden. Slice the duck breasts thinly crosswise on a bias. Using a slotted spoon, mound a serving of cabbage in the center of each plate and arrange the duck slices on top. Top with the dumplings, dividing them evenly.

"My dad used to love this dish, so my mom would make it. It makes me think of home."

STEFAN, SEASON 5

Q + A

WITH
stefan

Stefan Richter seemed to be the chef to beat during Season 5. He won the most challenges and consistently demonstrated his skills as an all-around chef, making everything from a simple minestrone to soulful European food to complex desserts. Stefan and Fabio bonded to form Team Europe; their dual interviews and cute banter pretty much stole the show. Perhaps Stefan was just a little too cocky going into the finale, where he wound up losing to rival Hosea. But don't cry for Stefan—he has landed on his feet, and is still as cocky as ever.

What are you up to these days?

I have a new restaurant, Stefan's, at L.A. Farm in Santa Monica. We do sexy food. I've lived everywhere, so I take things from all over. I'm still catering and consulting, and I'm shooting a new TV show.

Your plating was impressive throughout the competition. What advice would you give about plating and presentation?

First of all, take all the stupid Fiesta ware and throw it away. Why do a beautiful dish and put it on a frickin' green plate? Also, if you make nice food, make sure you keep it nice and tight in the middle of the plate; it should be centered on the plate. Make good food, and make it simple. If you make a family meal, make three or four good items, don't make sixty items. And forget the garnish. If you're going to use a garnish, it needs to be edible. No rosemary sprigs on the plate.

Speaking of inedible garnishes, you put a rose on your plate.

That was different . . . that was for Padma.

Who did you really admire of your castmates?

Leah and Jamie. I love Jamie and Leah is a great chef.

You made a delicious cabbage as part of your Roasted Duck with Pretzel Dumplings (page 57). What are some of your braising tips?

The most important thing is not to rush the braise. And use your senses—smell, sight, touch, and taste—to know when it is done, not the clock.

What is the new trend in dining these days?

Back to basics is key. People go to restaurants, they want to eat food. The whole molecular gastronomy thing is going to die out. Liquid balls of mozzarella—who wants to eat that?

You've said you were happy you didn't win the Top Chef title. What did you mean?

I look like a million bucks. I come off the show and look like a great chef, not "that *Top Chef* guy."

What advice would you give to future chef'testants?

Go on the show, and think, *What do you want to be seen as?* That's who you should be.

Q + A

WITH
kevin

Kevin Gillespie, chef-owner of Woodfire Grill in Atlanta, won the first Elimination Challenge of Season 6 with his Oil-Poached Arctic Char (page 109), and continued to bring his A game to every challenge, making it all the way to the finale in Napa. With his affable, low-key persona and passion for pork, Kevin won the hearts and bellies of viewers around the nation with his homey-yet-sophisticated fare, eventually taking home the title of Fan Favorite.

How did your experience on *Top Chef* compare to your expectations going in?

It was way more challenging than I had expected. The show really challenges your endurance and ability to handle stress and keep your mind focused, despite crazy things happening around you. To be successful on the show, it's not enough to be a great cook. It's critical that you're able to think on your feet.

What has the reaction been like since the show started airing?

It's insane. The restaurant is fully booked every night. On a personal level, people come up and speak to me everywhere. People feel like they know you. If they are from Atlanta or the South, they feel like I am up there representing them. It's nice to know people are standing behind you, and it made me want to bring it home for the South. People are proud to be from here, and they want other people to know that there are legitimate chefs down here.

What was it like eating at the table with all those amazing French chefs in Episode 4?

It was one of the most stressful moments of my entire life. I was sitting with people whom I know from books, and whom I've looked up to my whole life. Add to that the fact that I was a competitor eating my fellow competitors' food, while the judges ripped it apart. The judges would ask my opinion, and I felt

stymied. I was like, "Um, I'm not 100 percent sure. . . ." I hadn't brought a full suit, and Daniel Boulud said to me, "Make sure you wear a suit." So I had to go out that day with the producers and buy one. Very stressful.

What made you want to become a chef?

I wanted to be a cook even as a little kid. I grew up in Locust Grove, Georgia, and food was very important in my family. We all lived near one another, and every morning, my whole extended family ate breakfast at my grandmother's house. Every family function revolved around a meal, and everyone contributed. I felt a connection to that. I made my grandmother teach me how to cook. Academics was also very important to me, but then I had an epiphany that it was not the right choice for me.

Your cooking is very technically advanced. How did you learn to cook like that?

I believe in extremely precise technique. Whatever you do, it should be done the right way. Making grits, for example. Everyone in the South eats grits, and yet more often than not, they're terrible because people don't source the best grits and don't take the time to cook it the right way. I hope that my technical proficiency and also my personal connection to the food come through. Some people's food has no soul; it's cold. I try to walk that fine line between the two.

KEVIN'S MEATBALLS IN HEARTY TOMATO SAUCE

MEATBALLS

8 ounces ground beef

6 ounces ground lamb

6 ounces ground pork

1 cup finely diced white bread

1/4 cup heavy cream

1 large egg

1 tablespoon Madeira wine

1 teaspoon ground fennel or crushed fennel seeds

1/4 teaspoon ground cinnamon

1 teaspoon salt

1/4 teaspoon freshly ground pepper

Vegetable oil for deep-frying

....

TOMATO SAUCE

Sofrito (below)

1/4 cup Madeira wine

One 28-ounce can tomato purée

1 sprig fresh marjoram

1 sprig fresh basil

1 sprig fresh thyme

2 bay leaves

Salt and freshly ground pepper

1 cup veal glace

1 cup chicken stock or low-sodium broth

....

Soft polenta (page 65) for serving

Chopped fresh basil and grated *pecorino romano* cheese for garnish

---

SERVES 4 TO 6

FOR THE MEATBALLS: Line 1 baking sheet with parchment paper and another with paper towels. In a large bowl, gently combine the beef, lamb, pork, bread, cream, egg, wine, fennel, cinnamon, salt, and pepper until thoroughly mixed. Shape the mixture into about thirty-five 1 1/2-inch balls and place them on the parchment-lined baking sheet.

Pour about 2 inches of oil into a large, heavy skillet and heat over medium-high heat until shimmering. Working in batches to avoid crowding, place the meatballs in the hot oil and fry, turning carefully, until golden brown on all sides, about 5 minutes total. Drain on the paper towel–lined baking sheet and set aside.

FOR THE TOMATO SAUCE: Cook the *sofrito* in a large pot as directed. Pour in the Madeira, scraping up any browned bits from the bottom of the pot. Add the tomato purée, marjoram, basil, thyme, and bay leaves. Season with salt and pepper. Pour in the veal glace and stock and stir to combine. Raise the heat to medium-high, bring to a simmer, and add the meatballs. Reduce the heat, cover, and simmer gently for at least 45 minutes or up to 3 hours. Remove the bay leaves and herb sprigs from the sauce. Taste and adjust the seasoning.

To serve, spoon the meatball sauce over the polenta. Sprinkle the basil and pecorino cheese over the top.

🕐 **Prep time:** 1 hour, or up to 3 hours for a long-cooking sauce

🖥 Season 6, Episode 10

🔥 **Quickfire Challenge:** Make a TV dinner based on a television series.

HOW TO MAKE

sofrito

2 tablespoons olive oil

1 medium onion, cut into brunoise

2 ribs celery, cut into brunoise

1 carrot, peeled and cut into brunoise

2 cloves garlic, minced

In a large pot, heat the olive oil over medium-high heat. Add the onion and sauté until translucent, about 10 minutes. Add the celery and carrot and continue to sauté for 5 minutes. Stir in the garlic and cook until all the vegetables are soft, about 5 minutes longer.

WITH
bryan and michael v.

Both master chefs and both insanely competitive, the Voltaggio brothers took sibling rivalry to a whole new level on Season 6. CIA-trained Bryan, the elder by just two years, is chef-owner of highly praised VOLT restaurant in Frederick, Maryland, while Michael has made his home across the country in Los Angeles, working in a series of top kitchens, most recently at the Dining Room at the Langham Hotel in Pasadena. Both were on top during the entire season, but it truly came down to the wire at the finale in Napa, where Michael's bold, wildly creative dishes won him the title of Top Chef.

What are you up to these days?

MICHAEL: Bryan's at McDonalds, working the French fry station. You're still doing that Bryan, right? Or did you move up to milk shake?

BRYAN: Oh, you're funny. Michael is working at Dairy Queen.

What was it like competing together? Have you always been competitive with each other?

BRYAN: We're friends and we're close, which was an advantage for us on the show. Obviously there was pressure because we were competing against each other, but there was also a level of support, which the other chef'testants didn't have.

MICHAEL: There's always a level of competition. We talk on the phone every day, and the first thing we say is, "What are you making today? How are you making that? Oh yeah? Well I'm making this." I want to make sure he's not doing something better than I am.

BRYAN: We're two brothers only two years apart, always one-upping each other. We're competitive by nature. We played a lot of sports growing up.

MICHAEL: He played soccer and I played football, which says something about us. You can tell Bryan's a little more feminine and I'm a little bit more masculine. Bryan, don't be mad.

What was it like to live together in such close quarters after all these years?

BRYAN: I was pretty excited about that. We're both chefs in different cities pretty far apart, and we hadn't been in the same city for the last fifteen years. It was really cool to be able to spend a good amount of time with him.

MICHAEL: We missed out on our twenties. We didn't go to college, we didn't party hard—we worked in the kitchen. So it was fun to let loose. We also had Mike I., who's a friend of mine. When the lights went out and the cameras were gone, we were like children, laughing and joking and throwing stuff at one another. It was like a slumber party each night.

How did you both keep focused on the cooking?

BRYAN: You're in Las Vegas, in this great house, and everyone wants to have a good time, so it's difficult. I thought about why I was there, which was to cook and compete and try to win. I spent a lot of time planning the next day, looking through my ingredient list and trying to remember dishes I wanted to put together.

MICHAEL: When you're in a competition like this there's no time for emotions. You need to wake up and be focused and get the job done. That's not the criteria for just the show—that's the criteria for what we do every day.

What do you admire about each other's food and craft?

MICHAEL: Bryan is probably one of the most solid technicians I've ever seen. His basic skills are cleaner and more developed than most. Second to that—and Bryan, don't listen to this because your head's going to explode—he's not just a great cook, he's a great chef. He understands the business. I focused more on food my entire career; I've always been a great cook. I could learn a lot more about being a chef from Bryan.

BRYAN: As a result, Michael can do some pretty incredible things. He's done things that I've never seen applied to food. His craft is a little bit more modern. He's very innovative and definitely a trendsetter; that's really cool. And he's very driven.

What do you like to do when you're not cooking?

BRYAN: My cooks sleep on their days off. On my days off, I want to be outside because I spend so much time in the kitchen already. I spend time with my family, my two-year-old boy.

MICHAEL: It's important to do things outside of the kitchen so you have a life outside the kitchen and so you don't resent the fact that you spend sixteen hours a day behind a fire. I have two daughters; they are a priority.

Who would win in an arm-wrestling match?

BRYAN: Me.

MICHAEL: Bryan. But I would win a fight, hands down. Bryan has better form and tactic. Here's the thing: Bryan's like a trained boxer, and I'm just a street fighter. So he's going to get his licks in, and I'm just going to fight as dirty as I have to to win.

BRYAN'S PORK CHOPS WITH LEMONY GREENS

WINNER!

PORK CHOPS

4 center-portion pork loin chops, about 5 ounces each

2 teaspoons Maldon sea salt

1/2 cup olive oil, plus more for rubbing

1 tablespoon coarsely ground pepper

1/2 teaspoon smoked paprika

1/2 teaspoon cumin seeds, crushed

12 sprigs fresh thyme

2 sprigs fresh rosemary

2 cloves garlic

1 shallot, sliced

....

GREENS

1 tablespoon unsalted butter

1/3 cup diced red onion

2 large bunches dandelion greens, escarole, or Swiss chard

Grated zest of 1 lemon

Salt and freshly ground pepper

....

Soft Polenta (below) for serving (optional)

SERVES 4

FOR THE PORK CHOPS: Season the pork chops with the sea salt.

In a large baking dish, combine the 1/2 cup olive oil with the pepper, paprika, cumin, thyme, rosemary, garlic, and shallot. Mix well. Add the pork chops to the marinade, turning to coat. Cover with plastic wrap and marinate in the refrigerator for at least 4 hours or up to overnight.

Preheat a grill or broiler to medium-high.

Remove the chops from marinade and pat dry thoroughly with paper towels. Rub each chop with olive oil. Arrange the chops directly over the fire or under the broiler about 4 inches from the heat source and sear for about 2 minutes on each side.

Move the pork away from the direct fire and continue cooking until a meat thermometer inserted in the thickest part registers 150°F, 5 to 10 minutes longer. Remove from the grill, tent loosely with aluminum foil, and let rest for 5 to 10 minutes.

FOR THE GREENS: In a sauté pan, melt the butter over medium-high heat. Add the onion and sauté until golden, about 10 minutes. Add the greens and lemon zest and sauté until the greens are wilted, about 10 minutes. Remove from the heat and season with salt and pepper.

To serve, mound a portion of greens on each plate. Place a pork chop on top of the greens. Spoon some polenta alongside or pass at the table, if you like.

Prep time: 1 hour, plus marinating

Season 6, Episode 5

Elimination Challenge: Prepare a lunch dish for cowboys on a ranch using fire pits and limited supplies.

HOW TO MAKE

soft polenta

5 cups milk or water

1 cup coarse polenta

4 tablespoons unsalted butter

Salt and freshly ground pepper

In a large saucepan, bring the milk to a boil over high heat. Gradually whisk in the polenta. Reduce the heat to low and continue stirring with a wooden spoon until the polenta is thick and pulls away from the sides of the pan, about 40 minutes. Stir in the butter and season to taste with salt and pepper, and/or optional seasonings such as herbs, cheeses, or lemon zest.

RICHARD B.'S COFFEE-BRAISED PORK SHOULDER

PORK SHOULDER

6 tablespoons barbecue seasoning or rub

4 tablespoons ground coffee

3 pounds boneless pork shoulder, cut into 6 equal pieces and patted dry

1 or 2 tablespoons canola oil

1 carrot, peeled and cut into small dice

1 large onion, cut into small dice

2 cloves garlic, minced

2 star anise pods

2 fresh or dried chile peppers, seeded and chopped

Salt and freshly ground pepper

1 cup cider vinegar

4 cups veal, duck, or chicken stock or low-sodium broth

BRAISED GREENS

1/4 cup chopped bacon or 2 tablespoons bacon fat

1/2 onion, minced

1 clove garlic, minced

Salt and freshly ground pepper

1 bunch Swiss chard, stemmed and cut into chiffonade

Hot pepper vinegar for serving

🕐 Prep time: 3 hours, plus marinating

📺 Season 4, episode 13

🔪 Elimination Challenge: Butcher a pig and use two different parts of it in two dishes.

SERVES 6

FOR THE PORK SHOULDER: Preheat the oven to 325°F. In a small bowl, combine the barbecue seasoning and coffee. Rub the mixture all over the pork. Refrigerate for at least 1 hour or up to 12 hours.

Line a baking sheet with paper towels. In a large sauté pan, heat the oil over medium-high heat and sear the pork on all sides until golden brown, about 15 minutes. Blot the pork dry on the paper towels. If the fond is black, wash out the pan and add fresh oil.

Add the carrot and onion to the pan and sauté until brown, about 2 minutes. Add the garlic and sauté for 1 minute. Stir in the star anise, chiles, and salt and pepper to taste. Cook until the star anise and chiles are toasted. Add the vinegar and stir to scrape up the browned bits from the bottom of the pan. Return the pork to the pan, then add the stock and bring to a boil. Reduce the heat to low and simmer until the meat is fork-tender, about 2 hours. Transfer the pork to a plate and tent with aluminum foil. Strain the liquid through a sieve into a clean saucepan. If the sauce is thick enough to suit you, keep it warm. If it is too thin, cook to reduce it over medium heat.

FOR THE BRAISED GREENS: In a medium sauté pan, sweat the bacon or warm the fat over medium-high heat. Add the onion and garlic and cook until translucent, about 5 minutes. Season with salt and pepper. Add the chard and cook until the greens are bright and slightly tender, about 5 minutes. Remove from the heat. Splash a little vinegar on the greens just before serving.

To serve, slice the pork. Place a mound of braised greens on each plate. Top them with several pieces of pork and spoon the sauce over the meat.

SPIKE'S BURGER DEMO

One of the stars of Season 4, Spike Mendelsohn made a mark with his colorful personality. Raised in his family's restaurants and trained at the CIA, Spike has a rock-star-chef attitude and the classical culinary training to back it up. Since appearing on *Top Chef*, Spike has made several high-spirited guest appearances on the show, and opened a successful burger place in Washington, D.C., called Good Stuff Eatery. He shares his secrets for making America's favorite sandwich.

HOW TO PREPARE A BURGER

1. Begin with a blend of very good-quality meat. I use a blend of chuck, short rib, and brisket that is 25 percent fat. Shape it into a patty about 3 inches thick.

2. Sear the patty in a hot pan for about 3 minutes; once it has a nice crust, flip it and sear for another 20 seconds.

3. Remove the burger from the pan and let rest until almost ready to serve, or for at least a few minutes.

4. When ready to serve, throw it back in the hot pan for another 45 seconds or longer, depending whether you want it rare or medium-rare.

5. At this point, add bacon and other toppings.

6. Cover with cheese and put a lid on to help it melt.

7. Butter both sides of a potato bun and toast it on both sides on a hot frying pan.

8. Assemble the burger on the toasted bun. Top with lettuce, tomato, onion, and/or mayonnaise.

9. Wrap it in waxed paper and serve.

- Everyone lets meat rest when it comes to steak and chops, but they get lazy with burgers. You have to let them rest in order to redistribute the juices evenly.

"I can tell from ten feet away if the steak is rare, medium-rare, or well just by the sound the meat is making in the pan."

COOKING PHILOSOPHY: You can have the best technique in the world, but at the end of the day, if you're not having fun, what's the point? Food is about bringing people around a table to have fun.

NEXT BIG PROJECT: I'm opening a New York–style pizza joint in Washington, D.C.

ON THE PERFECT CHEESE: American cheese is underrated. It's actually a perfect cheese for a burger.

GO-TO COMFORT FOOD: Roast chicken. I halve potatoes and roast them underneath the chicken so they soak.

RICK BAYLESS'S QUESO FUNDIDO BURGERS

★★★
TOP CHEF MASTERS
WINNER!

TRIO OF GUACAMOLES

6 large, ripe avocados, halved and pitted

2/3 cup fresh cilantro leaves, finely chopped

1/2 red onion, minced, rinsed, and drained

Juice of 1 lime

Salt

1/2 small mango, peeled and cut into small dice

1/2 small jicama, peeled and cut into small dice

1/3 cup toasted pumpkin seeds, finely ground

2 large tomatoes, quartered

1 serrano chile, seeded and coarsely chopped

QUESO FUNDIDO BURGERS

Vegetable oil for greasing, plus 2 tablespoons

2 pounds ground chuck or rib eye

1 teaspoon chipotle chile powder

Salt

8 ounces Mexican chorizo, casings removed

1 red onion, sliced into 1/4-inch rings

2 poblano or Anaheim chiles

8 thick slices Monterey Jack cheese

4 brioche buns, toasted

SERVES 4

FOR THE GUACAMOLES: Scoop the flesh from the avocados into a large bowl and mash until fairly smooth. Mix in the cilantro, onion, and lime juice and season with salt. Divide among 3 bowls. Mix the mango and jicama into the first bowl. Mix the pumpkin seeds into the second bowl. In a food processor, finely chop the tomatoes and chile, then stir them into the third bowl.

FOR THE BURGERS: Preheat a grill to medium-high and lightly oil the grill rack. In a medium bowl, gently mix the ground beef with the chile powder and a pinch of salt until well combined. Divide the meat into 4 equal portions and form into patties.

Heat a skillet over medium-high heat. Add the chorizo and stir to break up any chunks. Cook until the meat is no longer pink, about 10 minutes. Remove from the heat and set aside.

Toss the onion rings with 1 tablespoon of the oil and salt to taste. Place on the grill and cook, turning occasionally until browned, 2 to 3 minutes per side. Grill the chiles until blackened and blistered, about 10 minutes. Transfer them to a paper bag to steam for 5 minutes, then peel, seed, and slice into 1/4-inch-wide strips.

Grill the burgers for 3 minutes on each side. Top each patty with a slice of cheese, one-fourth of the chorizo, and another slice of cheese. Grill to melt the cheese.

To serve, place each burger on the bottom half of a toasted bun and top with the onions and chiles. Close with the bun tops and serve with the guacamoles.

🕐 Prep time: 1 hour

🖥 *Top Chef Masters,* Season 1, Episode 8

🔥 Quickfire Challenge: Make a gourmet hamburger.

JENNIFER C.'S SKIRT STEAK SALAD

MARINADE

1 tablespoon hoisin sauce

1 tablespoon *sambal oelek*

1/4 cup soy sauce

1 teaspoon molasses

Grated zest and juice of
3 or 4 oranges (about 1 cup juice)

2 cloves garlic, thinly sliced

One 2-inch piece fresh ginger, peeled
and thinly sliced

2 tablespoons finely chopped
fresh cilantro

2 tablespoons finely chopped
fresh Thai basil

....

1 skirt steak, about 1 pound

Vegetable oil for greasing

....

SALAD

3 Asian pears

4 heads bok choy, blanched and
shocked (see page 15), drained and
cut into strips

11/2 fennel bulbs, trimmed, cored, and
thinly sliced

8 mandarin oranges, supremed

Juice of 1 lime

....

VINAIGRETTE

Juice of 6 limes

1/4 cup rice vinegar

1/4 cup canola oil

1 scallion, white part only, thinly sliced

Salt and freshly ground pepper

🕐 **Prep time:** 45 minutes,
plus marinating

🖵 Season 6, Episode 7

🔪 Elimination Challenge:
Create a dish using only
surprise ingredients.

SERVES 4

FOR THE MARINADE: In a small bowl, mix together the hoisin, *sambal*, soy sauce, molasses, orange zest and juice, garlic, ginger, cilantro, and basil. Reserve 1/4 cup of the marinade and pour the rest into a baking dish. Put the steak in the marinade and turn to coat. Marinate for 11/2 hours in the refrigerator.

Preheat a grill to high and lightly oil the grill rack. Remove the steak from the marinade and place on the grill. Cook until medium-rare, turning 2 or 3 times and basting each side twice with the reserved marinade, about 6 to 8 minutes total. Remove from the grill and let rest while you prepare the salad.

FOR THE SALAD: Slice the pears in half and grill until soft, turning once, about 4 minutes total. Remove from the heat and cut into batonnets, discarding the stems and cores. Place in a bowl and add the fennel, oranges, and lime juice. Set aside.

FOR THE VINAIGRETTE: In a small bowl, whisk together the lime juice and vinegar. Continuing to whisk, slowly drizzle in the oil until emulsified. Add the scallion and season to taste with salt and pepper. Drizzle the vinaigrette over the salad and toss to coat evenly.

To serve, thinly slice the steak against the grain and arrange a portion in the center of each plate. Place a serving of salad on top of the meat.

Q + A

jennifer c.

This bright young chef from Philadelphia had a roller-coasted ride of a season. Jennifer Carroll started off with a bang, winning the first Season 6 Quickfire with her Clam Ceviche (page 85), only to flag mid-season, when she hit a wall of stress and exhaustion. But instead of going home early, Jennifer re-emerged, Phoenix-like, with a very strong fourth-place finish. She was respected by her castmates for her technical skill and her strong leadership in the kitchen.

Who has been your biggest culinary influence?

Eric Ripert has definitely been the biggest influence on me. When I moved to New York after school, I went to Le Bernardin and got hired there. The way it works in the Le Bernardin kitchen is, you start at the bottom and work your way up, so you learn every single aspect of the kitchen from the bottom up. Eric taught me how to challenge my palate and look for the complexity and subtlety. He taught me to let the ingredients be the star of the plate; it's our job to elevate that and bring out the best it can be.

What's life after Top Chef like?

We have been really busy at Ten Arts. A lot of people have been coming in because of the show, and that has brought a whole new energy to the restaurant. People recognize me all the time, and people were supporting me, saying "Go Philly."

What was your experience like being on Top Chef?

It was amazing. It's a lot harder than what it looks like, so much more emotional than when you're watching it on TV. You are sleep deprived and stuck living with people you don't know, so you form an instant bond with other people. Everyone got along really well. I was close to Ashley, and Mike I. was just a complete jokester. I mean, he's obnoxious and loud, but also funny and

wonderful. I got along with both the brothers. And Kevin and I had a lot in common in terms of cooking, and also personality and outlook. I'm in touch with pretty much everyone.

You started out incredibly strong, but as the season wore on you seemed to flag. What happened?

I became a little unfocused. I was definitely stressed out, and when I couldn't do what I wanted to do absolutely perfectly, it was just really bothering me. I was beating myself up, and it affected my performance. The show is a totally unreal situation, with no downtime. You're always on edge, and I guess I didn't react well to that.

Did you learn anything from working with these other young chefs?

Michael V. and Bryan and Mike I. were pulling out some crazy techniques that I had never seen before, and it inspired me and made me want to learn about molecular gastronomy. I've never used liquid nitrogen before, and I'm still kind of afraid of it, but that is so cool. Also, the gels and the pearls—there are so many different things you can do.

What advice do you have for future chef'testants?

Stay true to who you are, stay true to your style. Don't get caught up in the drama. Stay focused.

HOSEA'S HOISIN-BRAISED SHORT RIBS

3 pounds boneless beef short ribs

Salt and freshly ground pepper

2 tablespoons vegetable oil

1 cup chopped onion

1 cup peeled and chopped carrots

1 cup chopped celery

1/4 cup tomato paste

1 cup dry red wine

2 cups beef stock or low-sodium broth

1 1/2 cups hoisin sauce

1/4 cup firmly packed brown sugar

3/4 cup fresh orange juice

2 cups water

Leaves from 1 bunch fresh thyme, a few whole sprigs reserved

SERVES 4

Pat the short ribs dry and season with salt and pepper. In a Dutch oven or other heavy-bottomed ovenproof pot, heat 1 tablespoon of the oil over medium-high heat. Sear the short ribs to brown them on all sides, 2 to 3 minutes per side, and remove them from the pan. Set aside.

Preheat the oven to 325°F.

Add the remaining 1 tablespoon oil to the pot. Add the onion, carrots, and celery and sauté until caramelized, 10 to 12 minutes. Push aside the onion mixture, add the tomato paste, and brown for 2 or 3 minutes. Mix in the onion mixture, add the red wine, and stir to scrape up the browned bits from the bottom of the pot. Reduce the sauce until slightly thickened, about 5 minutes. Add the beef stock, hoisin, brown sugar, orange juice, water, and thyme leaves and bring to a simmer. Put the ribs back into the pot, cover, and transfer to the oven. Braise the ribs until they are very tender, about 3 hours, checking on the pot and stirring every hour.

Transfer the ribs to a platter and keep warm. Strain the sauce through a fine-mesh sieve into a medium saucepan. Taste and adjust the seasoning, then reheat the sauce.

To serve, divide the short ribs among 4 dinner plates. Top with the sauce and garnish with the thyme sprigs.

Prep time: 4 hours

Season 5, Episode 9

Elimination Challenge:
Restaurant Wars— open a restaurant for dinner service.

BRAISING RIBS

Braised short ribs have become so popular that they are virtually ubiquitous in restaurants. They are hearty, savory, and delicious, and can be combined with any number of flavors. If you're in the mood for a classic braise, use traditional aromatics, beef stock, and a deep red wine. If you are in the mood for a zestier recipe, substitute garlic and ginger for carrot and celery, and add other Asian ingredients to the braising liquid.

"I love Hosea. He is a sweet guy and I can't wait to kick his ass skiing or in a cook-off in his restaurant."

STEFAN, SEASON 5

SPIKE'S TOMAHAWK CHOP

SWEET POTATO PURÉE

8 medium sweet potatoes

1½ cups (3 sticks) unsalted butter, at room temperature

1 tablespoon honey

1 teaspoon brown sugar

Salt and freshly ground pepper

CIPOLLINI AND BRUSSELS SPROUT SALAD

20 small cipollini or pearl onions, peeled

2 pounds Brussels sprouts, trimmed and leaves separated

Extra-virgin olive oil for drizzling

Salt and freshly ground pepper

TOMAHAWK CHOPS

3 tomahawk chops or frenched bone-in rib-eye steaks, about 2 pounds each

Extra-virgin olive oil for brushing

Salt and freshly ground pepper

SERVES 6 TO 8

FOR THE SWEET POTATO PURÉE: Preheat the oven to 425°F. Pierce the sweet potatoes with a fork in several places and bake until tender, 50 to 60 minutes. Set aside to cool slightly. Cut open the potatoes, scoop out the cooked flesh, and put in a bowl. Add the butter, honey, and brown sugar and, using an electric mixer, beat until smooth. Season with salt and pepper. Set aside and keep warm.

FOR THE CIPOLLINI AND BRUSSELS SPROUT SALAD: Raise the oven temperature to 450°F. Arrange the onions on a baking sheet and roast, turning at least once to brown both sides, until tender, about 30 minutes.

Meanwhile, blanch and shock the Brussels sprouts leaves (see page 15), then drain. In a large bowl, combine the cipollini onions with the Brussels sprout leaves. Toss with a little olive oil and season with salt and pepper.

FOR THE TOMAHAWK CHOPS Preheat a grill to high for indirect-heat grilling. (If cooking on the stove top, place a heavy grill pan or skillet over medium-high heat and preheat the oven to 350°F.)

Just before grilling, brush both sides of the chops with olive oil and season with salt and pepper. Arrange the chops directly over the heat and grill for 2 minutes on each side. Transfer to the indirect heat side of the grill. Cover the grill and finish cooking the chops until a meat thermometer registers the desired doneness, 120°F for rare or 130°F for medium-rare. (If cooking on the stove top, sear the chops for 2 minutes on each side, then transfer to the oven and cook to the desired doneness.) Transfer to a platter and tent with aluminum foil. Let rest for 5 minutes before serving.

To serve, slice the chops. Pass the sweet potato purée and salad separately.

⏱ **Prep time:** 2 hours

🖥 Season 4, Episode 12

🔪 **Elimination Challenge:**
Create an appetizer and entrée to be made in Rick Tramonto's restaurant.

ABOUT AN INGREDIENT

tomahawk chops

"Tomahawk chop" is the name given to a bone-in beef rib chop. It's so called because once it has been frenched, a beef rib chop resembles a Native American tomahawk, or axe. It's not a common fixture on menus these days, but these mammoth, almost Flintstonian chops make occasional appearances at steakhouses and are priced at a premium.

ARIANE'S LAMB DEMO

On Season 5, Ariane Duarte experienced some extreme highs and lows, at times thrilling and other times disappointing the judges with her homey food. She won the challenge for Gail's bridal shower with her perfectly cooked rack of lamb, only to be eliminated later for a badly butchered lamb leg in the On the Farm Elimination. Along the way, this down-to-earth chef of CulinAriane became a favorite of viewers and a kind of den mother to the other chefs.

"What I did wrong in the On the Farm episode—that show gets to your head! You get distracted by what everyone else wants to do. The baby lamb should have been roasted whole. Rosemary, garlic, salt, and pepper, and that's it. "

COOKING WITH FAMILY: My daughters scale and fillet fish with me, and they decorated all my Valentine's Day cookies for me.

MAGIC INGREDIENT: Fleur de sel.

SIGNATURE DISH: I brine air-chilled chicken that comes from Pennsylvania. We make an Earl Grey tea brine.

HOW TO PREPARE A RACK OF LAMB

As Ariane explains it, the trick to cooking rack of lamb is in the timing and in letting the meat rest. "Rack of lamb should be served medium-rare, and it should not taste gamey."

1. Clean the rack of lamb by frenching the bones and trimming excess fat.

2. Season the lamb well with salt and pepper.

3. Sear the lamb on all sides over medium-high heat until it is nicely browned.

4. Place it in a 425°F oven for 8 minutes.

5. Remove from the oven and let rest for 8 to 10 minutes.

6. Return it to the oven for 5 minutes longer, until browned on the outside and still pink in the middle when cut into.

Ariane's Favorite Lamb Marinades

- Yogurt marinade with garlic and fresh thyme or fresh cilantro.
- Red-wine marinade with soy sauce, rosemary, and smashed garlic.

MICHAEL CHIARELLO'S BRAISED LAMB SHANK

4 lamb shanks, boned and trimmed of excess fat and sinew

2 teaspoons gray sea salt, plus more to taste

1 teaspoon fennel seeds, finely ground, plus 1 teaspoon whole seeds

1/2 teaspoon freshly ground pepper, plus more to taste

2 tablespoons extra-virgin olive oil

4 cloves garlic, minced

6 fennel bulbs, trimmed, cored, and sliced

1 onion, sliced

1/2 cup water

4 cups goat's milk

1/2 cup heavy cream

1 bay leaf

2 tablespoons chopped fresh flat-leaf parsley

SERVES 4

Season the lamb shanks with the sea salt, ground fennel seeds, and pepper. Heat the olive oil in a Dutch oven or heavy-bottomed pot over medium-high heat. Add the lamb and brown on all sides, about 5 minutes. Remove the lamb from the pot and pour out three-quarters of the fat. Return the pot to medium heat, add the garlic, and cook, stirring, for about 1 minute. Add the sliced fennel, onion, and whole fennel seeds and season with salt and pepper. Cook, stirring often, until the vegetables are soft and slightly browned, about 15 minutes.

Raise the heat to high, add the water, and scrape up any browned bits from the bottom of the pot. Return the browned lamb to the pot and add the milk, cream, and bay leaf. Bring to a simmer, then reduce the heat to maintain a bare simmer. Cover the pot and cook slowly on the stove top until the lamb is very tender, about 3 hours.

Remove from the heat and let cool for at least 15 minutes. Carefully remove the lamb pieces from the braising liquid. Discard the bay leaf. Using an immersion blender, or transferring in batches to a standing blender, purée the braising liquid until smooth. Stir in the parsley. Taste and adjust the seasoning with salt and pepper, if needed.

To serve, divide the shanks among 4 plates and accompany with the sauce.

Prep time: 4 hours

Top Chef Masters, Season 1, Episode 9

Elimination Challenge: Create a buffet for 200 guests with a team of three sous-chefs.

MICHAEL DISHES

"Braising in milk is an ancient technique in Italy. The goat's milk sweetens the meat and makes a really silken sauce. By the time the lamb has finished braising in the goat's milk and fennel, it all magically comes together. Osso buco is tradition-ally done with veal, but lamb has more flavor. Back in the 1980s, lamb shank was not yet a popular dish. I used to have to go to the farmers and get them to give me the shanks."

"I could eat Michael's food every day."

HAROLD, SEASON 1 WINNER

STEPHEN'S WINE-PAIRING DEMO

Perhaps no chef'testant has ever known as much about wine—and was as eager to share that knowledge—as Season 1's own Top Sommelier, Stephen Asprinio. In Season 3, he made a special appearance as a wine-pairing consultant for Restaurant Wars. Since leaving *Top Chef*, Stephen has opened his own restaurant and wine bar in Palm Beach called Forté di Asprinio.

"In pairing wine and food, the idea is to create a perfect balance between the different flavor characteristics of each, while still maintaining the individual integrity of both the wine and the food."

CURRENT AGENDA: Traveling around the United States and abroad, dining at new restaurants as much as possible, and constantly tasting wines.

BEST WINE EVER TASTED: 1978 Domaine de la Romanée-Conti from Burgundy, France

WINE I'D WANT AT MY LAST MEAL: Prestige Bubbles (Tête de Cuvée Champagne)

ADVICE FOR WINE LOVERS: Taste, taste, taste! The more exposure to new wines, the better the palate gets.

STEPHEN'S WINE-PAIRING DO'S & DON'TS

Do:

1. Drink Champagne with everything.

2. Pair food with sake. It's the most overlooked wine in the world.

3. Enjoy regional wines with regional cuisine.

4. Step outside the box and experiment with different food and wine pairings.

5. Remember that food can be paired with wines, not only the other way around.

Don't:

1. Drink red wine with raw oysters. Ever.

2. Only pair white wines with fish.

3. Only pair red wines with meat.

4. Only pair sweet wines with dessert.

5. Forget to have fun. It's just fermented grape juice.

Stephen's Special-Occasion Pairings:

- For a rainy day: A rich, smooth Syrah from Washington

- For a romantic date: Pink bubbles (rosé Champagne)

- For a celebration: First-Growth Bordeaux

- For a picnic in summer: Spanish Albariño

- For a dinner party: Pinot Noir from Santa Rita Hills

- If stuck on a desert island: Austrian Riesling

Here are Stephen's suggested wine pairings for some of the recipes:

SIDES, SALADS, STARCHES

Ariane's Tomato, Watermelon, and Feta Salad (page 15)
WINE: Rudera Chenin Blanc, Stellenbosch, South Africa 2005

Suzanne Tracht's Fried Shallot Rings (page 18)
WINE: Segura Viudas Cava, Brut Reserva Heredad, Spain NV

Hubert Keller's Mac and Cheese (page 39)
WINE: Alex Gambal, Fixin Blanc, Burgundy, France 2006

MEATS

Ariane's Orange-Brined Turkey Breast (page 55)
WINE: Valpane Barbera del Monferrato, Rosso Pietro, Piedmont, Italy 2005

Stefan's Roasted Duck with Pretzel Dumplings (page 57)
WINE: Betts & Scholl, Grenache "The Chronique" Barossa Valley, Australia 2006

Hosea's Hoisin-Braised Short Ribs (page 73)
WINE: Mapema Malbec, Mendoza, Argentina 2006

SEAFOOD

Hubert Keller's Citrus-Coriander Oysters (page 87)
WINE: Movia Sauvignon Blanc, Primorje, Slovenia 2006

Jamie's Seared Scallops with Fennel Cream (page 99)
WINE: Planeta, La Segreta Bianco, Sicily, Italy 2007

Nils Noren's Salmon with Napa Cabbage and Chorizo (page 111)
WINE: Melville "Estate" Pinot Noir, Santa Rita Hills, California 2007

GLOBAL FLAVORS

Rick Bayless's Vegan Corn Tamale (page 125)
WINE: Brundlmayer Grüner Veltliner, Berg Vogelsang, Kamptal, Austria 2007

Anita Lo's Soft-Scrambled Egg with Shiitakes (page 133)
WINE: Jean Milan Brut, Carte Blanche, Grand Cru Champagne, France NV

Radhika's Jerk Halibut with Mango Slaw (page 139)
WINE: Lucien Albrecht Pinot Gris, Cuvee Cecile, Alsace, France 2005

ADVANCED APPLICATIONS

Michael V.'s Nitro Gazpacho (page 152)
WINE: Jose Pariente Verdejo, Rueda, Spain 2008

Andrew's Squid Ceviche with Yuzu-Mint Glacier (page 167)
WINE: Zilliken Kabinett Riesling, Saarburger Rausch, Mosel, Germany 2007

DESSERTS

Jeff's Lavender Crème Brûlée (page 187)
WINE: Pilliteri Estates Chardonnay Icewine, Ontario, Canada 2007

Carla's Nectarine and Strawberry Tartlets (page 195)
WINE: Massolino Moscato d'Asti, Piedmont, Italy 2008

Stephanie's Gorgonzola Cheesecake (page 203)
WINE: Chapoutier Banyuls, Roussillon, France 2007

SEAFOOD ESSENTIALS: SCALLOPS TO CEVICHE

107

99

91

95

87

WITH
eric ripert

Acclaimed French chef Eric Ripert has brought seafood to a new level of sophistication and elegance at his three-Michelin-star restaurant Le Bernardin in New York. When he graces the Judges' Table of *Top Chef*, he brings with him a sense of gravitas and expertise, as well as his generous and gracious persona. Chef Ripert made his first appearance for the Nestlé Chocolatier Quickfire Challenge during Season 2, and returned for the finale of Season 3 in Aspen, in which the chef'testants cooked trout for him over camping stoves. For the finale of Season 4, he gamely donned his whites and briefly acted as sous-chef to winner Stephanie, and in Season 5, he oversaw the Fish Fillet Quickfire Challenge and also opened his restaurant kitchen to the chef'testants, who were challenged to copy a few of his complex dishes.

What do you love most about the show?

I love that it is a fifty-fifty split of entertainment and good cooking, with a lot of integrity. If your dish sucks, you lose—it doesn't matter how good looking or funny you are. If the judging is not fair, the show loses credibility. Tom is a highly recognized professional chef, and Padma brings a lot of spice to the show, not just beauty but also knowledge and sophistication. Gail also has a great knowledge of food.

What do you think people can learn from watching the show?

A foodie who is watching the show will pick up more than a non-foodie. But the nice thing is that even someone who is not that into food and is watching for the entertainment will be introduced to new ingredients: "Oh, you can do something interesting with leeks" or "*That's* what fennel is." It inspires people to be curious and, down the line, to cook—not to duplicate the recipe they see on the show but to try their own thing. It's inspirational for a lot of people.

What are your criteria for judging?

The season is divided into two parts. If I know I'm going to be a judge in the semifinals and finals, I try not to watch the season until I am done; that way I have no preconceptions. I try not to have any opinion about their personalities. I judge by what is on the plate in front of me. Most of the time I don't know the struggle or drama they went through for the challenge. I am just looking at the harmony, the originality, and the flavor of the dish.

What's the biggest mistake that chef'testants make?

They try to complicate things too much. Also, they don't use common sense in terms of thinking about the context and the audience. For example, in Season 6 they had to cook on a ranch for cowboys. Imagine that you are in the desert where it's 110 degrees, and you are a cowboy with a big appetite in a rustic ambience. Do you really want to eat ceviche? I had to laugh when I saw that. You can do sophisticated rustic food, or maybe light food if it's so hot, but many of the chef'testants' dishes were not in sync with the challenge.

Who have been your favorite contenders from the various seasons?

During Season 5 we did a challenge at Le Bernardin, and I thought Stefan was very strong. He chose the lobster, and he executed it perfectly. I was impressed with his technique; I was rooting for him. At the end, it was a big surprise when he didn't win. In Season 4, I thought Stephanie would win. Not because I was her sous-chef. I liked what she was preparing. She had a good menu and she was executing it well. Jennifer C. is my chef in Philadelphia, and she's very talented. Of course I was rooting for her and hoped she would win the Season 6 title.

Would you ever compete on *Top Chef Masters*?

I didn't go on *Top Chef Masters* because, as much as I love to judge, cooking is more meditative for me. I like to take my time, and I like to cook what I want to cook. In a restaurant, you are under time pressure, and that is my job on a daily basis. So if I am going to do something outside of work, I need to not rush and to feel connected. As an analogy, I am a very good skier— I can ski in powder, do moguls, etc.—but I have never done a

competition because I would lose the sense of freedom I have when I ski. It would just kill the pleasure for me.

How would you describe your philosophy of food?

We have a mantra: the fish is the star of the plate. That completely dictates the cooking we do at Le Bernardin. We don't cook fish, we cook for the fish. Fish is so delicate, so you have to be very cautious not to bring in too many elements, not to overwhelm the star of the plate.

What are the most common mistakes people make when cooking fish?

First mistake is that they don't buy fresh fish. If it's not fresh, it's going to stink, and it's not going to be good. Then people have a tendency to overcook it and they end up with a stinky piece of cardboard.

))) TOP SEAFOOD (((

For some reason, seafood seems to bring a lot of drama to the *Top Chef* proceedings. Most chefs know their way around a fish, and yet seafood can be so delicate, so easy to mangle or overwhelm, that cooking it makes for exciting viewing.

Catch and Cook: Season 3, Episode 3

The chef'testants had to scoop their own shellfish out of a giant tank. In his excitement, Hung splashed water all over and ended up with a live crawfish on the floor.

Camping-Stove Trout: Season 3, Episode 14

The four finalists had to cook a trout dish outdoors over a camping stove in front of star seafood chef Eric Ripert. Casey managed to edge out seafood expert Brian M.

Top Scallop: Season 5, Episode 6

Before Jamie made her winning Seared Scallops with Fennel Cream (page 99), she was nearly sent home for her disappointing and slimy scallop *crudo*.

Battle of the Ceviches: Season 5, Episode 10

Though a ceviche maestro, Jeff was sent home for his overly complicated rock shrimp ceviche in the Super Bowl All Stars Challenge.

Eels, Glorious Eels: Season 5, Episode 11

In the Fish Fillet Challenge, seafood chef Hosea learned from Stefan that you have to nail an eel's head to a plank and then peel off its skin.

Aw Shucks: Season 6, Episode 1

In the Mise-en-Place Relay, Preeti tried to shuck all fifteen clams like oysters. Unfortunately, the methods are very different, and Preeti was unable to pry open her clams.

JENNIFER C.'S CLAM CEVICHE

WINNER!

24 clams, scrubbed

2 cups fresh lemon juice

2 cups fresh lime juice

1 cup cold water

4 sprigs fresh mint

4 sprigs fresh cilantro

2 sprigs fresh basil

¼ cup citron vinegar

2 tablespoons lemon oil

¼ small red onion, sliced

1 tomato, diced

Salt and ground Espelette pepper or smoked Spanish paprika

Pinch of tomato powder

SERVES 4

Shuck the clams over a bowl, catching the liquor. Remove the outer muscle and any sand from each clam, then slice razor thin and refrigerate until nearly ready to serve.

In a separate bowl, combine the lemon and lime juices, cold water, and reserved clam liquor.

Pick the leaves off the mint, cilantro, and basil sprigs. Reserve one-quarter of the leaves whole, then roughly chop the remaining three-quarters of the leaves and the stems. Add the chopped leaves and stems to the bowl of liquid. Stir in the citron vinegar, lemon oil, onion, and tomato. Season the ceviche base with salt and Espelette pepper, cover, and refrigerate for at least 2 hours or up to 8 hours.

Remove the ceviche base from the refrigerator and strain through a fine-mesh sieve into a medium bowl. Cut the reserved herb leaves into chiffonade and add half of them to the bowl, reserving the rest for garnish. Add the sliced clams to the ceviche base and adjust the seasoning as necessary.

To serve, spoon out the clams from the ceviche base onto individual plates. Sauce the plates with a small amount of the ceviche base and garnish with tomato powder and remaining fresh herb chiffonade.

Prep time: 30 minutes, plus chilling

Season 6, Episode 1

Quickfire Challenge:
Create a dish from an ingredient prepared in the Mise-en-Place Relay.

ABOUT AN INGREDIENT

tomato powder

Tomato powder is made from tomatoes that have been dried and ground to a fine powder. In this winning ceviche dish, just a pinch of the powder is used at the end to finish the dish with some sweet tomato flavor and attractive red color—part of a recent trend of savory dusting (see page 151).

> "Being in Las Vegas is crazy. I don't know if we're going to be cooking for magicians or feeding lions."
>
> JENNIFER C., SEASON 6

HUBERT KELLER'S CITRUS-CORIANDER OYSTERS

★★★
TOP CHEF MASTERS
WINNER!

1 teaspoon coriander seeds

4 cups rock salt

24 oysters, scrubbed

1 seedless orange

2 limes

3 tablespoons extra-virgin olive oil

1 teaspoon cracked black pepper

SERVES 4

In a small, dry sauté pan over medium heat, roast the coriander seeds until fragrant, about 2 minutes. Grind coarsely in a spice grinder or in a mortar with a pestle.

Spread a layer of rock salt on a sheet pan. Carefully shuck the oysters and set them on the rock salt. Alternatively, you can prepare a bed of crushed ice.

With a small, sharp knife, supreme the orange and cut each supreme in half cross-wise. Do the same to the limes.

To serve, garnish each oyster attractively with one-half supreme of orange and one-half supreme of lime. Drizzle the oysters with the olive oil and sprinkle them with the coriander and cracked pepper.

Prep time: 30 minutes

Top Chef Masters, Season 1, Episode 9

Elimination Challenge: Create a buffet for 200 guests with a team of three sous-chefs.

TOP CHEF MASTERS HOST

kelly choi dishes

"Hubert's eighteen-course feast was extraordinary, each course so delectable that it was intoxicating. In-your-face Vietnamese gazpacho, tender rack of lamb, marinated oysters, the tastiest beet salad ever, and a parade of nectarous desserts. It was a heart-stopping display of culinary perfection, tantalizing and gratifying all at once. I want to watch the footage of Hubert's cooking because I'm convinced he must have had a dozen more elves helping him."

"Chef Keller has very high standards, and he's very exacting."

TOM COLICCHIO, **CHEF AND HEAD JUDGE**

WITH
hubert keller

Born in the French region of Alsace, Hubert Keller is the virtuoso chef and owner behind Fleur de Lys and Burger Bar, both with locations in San Francisco and Las Vegas. Chef Keller has been involved with *Top Chef* since the very first Quickfire Challenge of the first episode, when he kicked Ken Lee off the line for dipping his finger in a sauce. After serving at the Judges' Table several times, Keller decided it was time to prove his own mettle as a competitor on *Top Chef Masters*. First he demonstrated a true chef's resourcefulness by draining his pasta in a dorm room shower, and then went on to create a succession of extraordinary dishes, including a decadent eighteen-course buffet and a delicious finale meal starring a *Baeckeoffe* reminiscent of his childhood.

How do you think the show has evolved?

When the producers approached us to shoot the first episode of Season 1 at Fleur de Lys, of course nobody had ever heard about *Top Chef*. I knew Tom Colicchio was on board, so that gave me confidence. A lot has changed since the first episode. The challenges are better thought out, they have a bigger budget, and the show has grown and become a monster—a good monster. At the first episode, none of us knew it would become such a hit.

As the show grew, the emphasis was really put more on the level of chef: more professional, more talented. At the beginning it was probably difficult to get a lot of chefs to go on the show, but now they are lining up to be a part of it, and the producers can be extremely selective.

You were a guest judge at the finales of Seasons 2 and 5. How do you eventually judge the winner?

I remember the one in Hawaii well. Marcel had done pretty good stuff all season, but the judges are judging just on that last competition. We had some expectations for Marcel, and that day was not his day. As a judge that's the tough part, because you follow

the chef'testants and you know their techniques, but it's like running in a race. It doesn't matter how fast or how well you've done in the past; it's all new each time.

Season 5 was a pretty close challenge. Both Hosea and Stefan were good, so it was a very close call. Tom gave Stefan a hard time because he froze the fish in his first course, but I liked it because it was a really cool technique. I think at that level when you get to the end, in reality, you are all winners. It almost comes down to the judges needing to find something wrong in order to pick a winner.

What made you want to compete on *Top Chef Masters*?

I have judged so many of them that I wanted to be part of it. I wanted to show that I could do that, too. With *Top Chef Masters*, we all had proven ourselves for years and years, so we basically entered all on the same starting line. We were even helping one another in the kitchen and hugging one another before going to Critics' Table, so the atmosphere was more one of professional respect and appreciation than of competition.

What was it like being on the other end as a competitor on *Top Chef Masters*?

If I were invited back to be a guest judge, I would still judge the same. But it was a little bit of an eye-opener to see what it really takes to pull off some of the challenges. Now I have a better idea of what the chef'testants go through. It's like an endurance test. Everything takes much longer than you can imagine. And you have the camera constantly on you; it takes a lot of guts to cook in front of the camera.

For me it was real. It was like when I'm in the kitchen. People have asked me if it felt new again, doing the prep and all that stuff by myself. It didn't. When you've done it for so long and that's your background, it's like riding a bike.

You also have your own television series. Do you think that experience helped you on *Top Chef Masters*?

Absolutely not. Honestly, when the challenge starts and the time is on, you forget about the camera. I was head down and absorbed in cooking as fast as I could. On *Top Chef*, there is no redoing it. On a regular cooking show, everything is done already, if there's a problem you just reshoot it or recook it.

What was it like sharing the kitchen with the other *Top Chef Masters* chefs?

It was an absolutely great experience. We all had a great relationship. We do charity events together, we see one another on different occasions. We had a good camaraderie going, and at the end, when the chefs would get cut, you would really feel it.

What was it like cooking the autobiographical meal for the finale?

I think it was the best challenge in all of *Top Chef*. We all loved it; it was exceptional. We were half expecting them to come in and throw another curve, but they really let us cook, let each of us show our originality. We were able to tell our story with food.

What is one food you can't live without?

Bread. I cannot have a meal without bread.

JENNIFER C.'S MUSSELS IN POTATO-LEMONGRASS BROTH

1/2 cup (1 stick) unsalted butter

1 tablespoon duck fat

4 cloves garlic, thinly sliced

1 shallot, thinly sliced

One 2- to 3-inch piece fresh ginger, peeled and thinly sliced

2 stalks lemongrass, tender bottom parts only, sliced

8 cups chicken stock or low-sodium broth

3 Yukon gold potatoes; 2 cut into 1/4-inch-thick slices, and 1 cut into batons 1/4 inch thick by 2 to 3 inches long

1/2 cup crème fraîche

Salt and freshly ground pepper

1 blue potato, finely diced

2 handfuls pea tendrils or mâche, spun dry

Salt and freshly ground black pepper

Ground Espelette pepper or sweet paprika

3 cups dry white wine

2 pounds mussels, scrubbed and debearded

Salt and freshly ground pepper

SERVES 6 AS A FIRST COURSE

In a medium saucepan, melt the butter with the duck fat over medium heat. Add the garlic, shallot, ginger, and lemongrass and sweat until tender, about 7 minutes. Pour the chicken stock into the pan and bring to a boil. Reduce the heat and simmer for 15 minutes.

Strain the broth through a fine-mesh sieve into a clean pot. Discard the solids. Put the pot over medium heat. Add the sliced potatoes and simmer until the potatoes are cooked through, about 10 minutes.

Transfer the potato mixture in batches to a blender and purée until smooth. Return the purée to the pot. Stir in the crème fraîche and season with salt and pepper. Set aside and keep warm.

Bring a pot of salted water to a simmer. Add the Yukon gold batons and finely diced blue potato and cook until tender, about 10 minutes. Drain and set the potatoes aside.

In a small bowl, season the pea tendrils with salt, black pepper, and Espelette pepper. Set aside.

In a medium sauté pan over medium-high heat, heat the wine to a low simmer. Add the mussels and sauté just until they open, about 5 minutes. Remove from the heat. Discard any unopened mussels.

To serve, place the seasoned pea tendrils in shallow bowls or on plates. Add potato purée, then a serving of mussels. Top the mussels with the potatoes. Pour 1/2 to 1 cup broth over each serving.

Prep time: 1 hour

Season 6, Episode 3

Quickfire Challenge: Create a dish using potatoes.

SUZANNE TRACHT'S RISOTTO WITH UNI

5 cups chicken stock or low-sodium broth

1 cup coconut water

1 tablespoon unsalted butter

1 cup Arborio or Carnaroli rice

1/2 cup dry white wine

4 ounces *uni* (sea urchin roe)

🕐 **Prep time:** 50 minutes

🖥 *Top Chef Masters*, Season 1, Episode 2

🔪 **Elimination Challenge:** Create a meal inspired by the television show *Lost*.

ABOUT AN INGREDIENT

uni

This creamy, briny sea urchin roe is a delicacy in Japan and growing in popularity elsewhere. Delicate *uni* is usually served as nigiri sushi, but here Suzanne Tracht adds it to her variety plate as part of a risotto.

SERVES 4 TO 6

In a medium saucepan, combine the chicken stock and coconut water over medium-low heat and bring to a bare simmer.

In a large saucepan over medium heat, melt the butter. Add the rice and stir to coat all the grains thoroughly. Sauté the rice until there is a slightly nutty aroma, 5 to 10 minutes. Add the wine, stirring until it is fully absorbed.

Add the broth slowly, 1 ladle at a time, allowing each addition to fully absorb before ladling more broth. Stir the rice often. Continue to cook the rice and ladle in broth until the risotto is rich and creamy but has some resistance to the tooth. Remove from the heat and gently stir in three-quarters of the *uni*, taking care not to crush the *uni*.

To serve, place a serving of risotto in the center of each plate and garnish with some of the remaining *uni*.

> "Foodies are fools for *uni*—that voluptuous texture, the sudden sense of sweetness as the briny scent of the sea fills your mouth."
>
> GAEL GREENE, *TOP CHEF MASTERS* CRITIC

ANTONIA'S PAPPARDELLE WITH LOBSTER AND SHRIMP

8 ounces medium shrimp, peeled and deveined, shells reserved

Meat from 1 lobster tail, cut into 1-inch cubes, shells reserved

2 teaspoons olive oil

2 shallots, cut into small dice

2 small onions, cut into small dice

2 cloves garlic, chopped, plus 1/4 cup chopped garlic

1 rib celery, cut into small dice

1 medium carrot, peeled and cut into small dice

4 tablespoons unsalted butter

1/2 teaspoon tomato paste

1 sprig fresh thyme

1 sprig fresh flat-leaf parsley

1 sprig fresh tarragon

2 cups dry white wine

1 cup water

Canola oil for deep-frying

1 pint cherry tomatoes

1/4 cup fresh opal basil leaves, cut into chiffonade

4 ounces squash blossoms

8 ounces dried pappardelle, or 1 pound fresh

SERVES 4

Place the shrimp and lobster meat in small, seperate bowls and set aside. Rinse the shells in cold water briefly and drain well. Chop the shells.

Heat the olive oil in a large, heavy skillet over medium-high heat. Add the seafood shells and sear for about 7 minutes. Reduce the heat to medium-high and add the shallots, onions, 2 cloves chopped garlic, celery, carrot, and 2 tablespoons of the butter. Cook until caramelized, about 15 minutes. Add the tomato paste, thyme, parsley, tarragon, and wine. Cook until thickened and reduced, about 10 minutes. Add the water, reduce the heat, and simmer gently for 5 minutes longer. Strain the seafood broth through a fine-mesh sieve into a clean saucepan and set aside.

Line a baking sheet with paper towels. Pour about 2 inches of oil into a heavy skillet and heat over medium-high heat until shimmering. Add the cherry tomatoes and fry until they pop and their skins loosen. Remove the tomatoes with a slotted spoon and transfer to the paper towels to drain. Let the tomatoes cool, peel, and then place them in a small bowl to marinate with the 1/4 cup chopped garlic and opal basil.

Bring a large pot of salted water to a boil. Meanwhile, remove the stems and small buds from inside the squash blossoms. Quarter the petals. Set aside. Add the pappardelle to the boiling water and cook until al dente, about 7 minutes. Drain.

In a large sauté pan, melt the remaining 2 tablespoons butter over medium-high heat. Add the marinated cherry tomatoes and seafood broth. Cook until a thick sauce forms, about 5 minutes. Add the lobster meat and stir for 1 minute. Add the shrimp and poach it in the liquid.

To serve, add the cooked pasta and squash blossoms and toss together.

Prep time: 1 hour, 30 minutes

Season 4, Episode 1

Elimination Challenge: Reinvent a classic dish against an opponent making the same dish.

RICK BAYLESS'S CHILE-GARLIC SHRIMP

Sweet Garlic Sauce (below)

1 pint fresh figs, quartered

1/2 cup almonds, toasted and chopped

2 limes

2 canned chipotle chiles in adobo sauce, drained, seeded, and cut into thin strips

Salt

2 pounds medium to large prawns (about 48 prawns), peeled and deveined (leaving the last joint and tail shell intact if desired)

3 tablespoons chopped fresh cilantro or flat-leaf parsley (optional)

SERVES 6

In a small saucepan, warm the garlic sauce over low heat. Remove and reserve 1 1/2 tablespoons of oil from the mixture, and add the figs and almonds to the pan.

Raise the heat to medium, squeeze the juice of 1 lime into the pan, and simmer until most of the juice has evaporated, about 5 minutes. Stir in the chiles, then taste and season with salt if necessary. Reduce the heat to low and keep the *mojo* warm.

Cut the remaining lime into 6 wedges and place in a small serving bowl.

In a large nonstick skillet, heat the 1 1/2 tablespoons reserved garlic oil over medium-high heat. Add half of the prawns to the skillet, sprinkle generously with salt, and gently stir or shake constantly until the prawns are just pink and opaque throughout, 3 to 4 minutes. Stir in half of the cilantro, if using. Remove from the heat and transfer the prawns to a deep serving platter. Repeat to cook the remaining prawns.

To serve, sauce the prawns with the *mojo* to taste and pass the lime wedges. (The *mojo* keeps for a couple of weeks in the refrigerator. The oil will solidify, but will liquefy again at room temperature. Warm cold *mojo* slowly over low heat before using.)

Prep time: 1 hour

Top Chef Masters, Season 1, Episode 9

Elimination Challenge: Create a buffet for 200 guests with a team of three sous-chefs.

HOW TO MAKE

sweet garlic sauce (*mojo de ajo*)

1 cup extra-virgin olive oil

1/2 cup chopped garlic (about 2 large heads)

1/2 teaspoon salt

In a small saucepan, combine the oil, garlic, and salt. Bring the mixture to the barest simmer over very low heat and cook, stirring occasionally, until the garlic is soft and golden, about 30 minutes.

"This experience was tough, amazing, incredible, overwhelming, lifetime friend-making, satisfying, tough."

RICK BAYLESS, *TOP CHEF MASTERS* SEASON 1 WINNER

WHEN THE STOVES ARE OFF

All work and no play makes for a dull chef. Things are fast and furious in the kitchen, so chefs need to unwind and get away from the flames once in a while. Check out these chef'testants' chosen pastimes, some more relaxing than others.

carla

"When we were doing the show I learned how to make friendship bracelets. Let me tell you, I've taken friendship bracelets to a whole new level."

hosea

"I play way too much poker. I take trips to Vegas for three days and don't sleep. If I were just a little bit better poker player I'd quit cooking because I'd make a lot more money."

hubert keller

"I've always loved music, and a friend got me into DJ'ing. I love the way you can influence an entire audience by changing the beat at the right moment. I make the playlists in all my restaurants."

dale t.

"I'm a gym shoe junkie. I'm obsessed with Jordans and Air Max 90s. I just moved in with my girlfriend, and I have more shoes than she does."

fabio

"I like gardening, fishing, skiing, riding motorcycles with one wheel off the ground, and shooting, especially if the target does not run away."

spike

"I like to be in the water, any water: bathtub, pool, lake, pouring rain, it doesn't matter. I throw these humongous pool parties at a hotel every Sunday."

jamie

"I am obsessive-compulsive when it comes to cleaning. I vacuum, I do everything before I leave the house."

bryan

"My Harley is probaby the biggest stress reliever."

JAMIE'S SCALLOP DEMO

This down-to-earth executive chef of Absinthe restaurant in San Francisco was a hit with audiences and judges during Season 5, when she was pegged as the Top Scallop lady for her repeated use of the mollusk. To be fair, Jamie can do a lot more than scallops, but she does have a great technique, which she used to win the Signature Dish Elimination with her Seared Scallops with Fennel and Cream (page 99).

HOW TO PREPARE SCALLOPS

It seems simple enough—sautéing scallops in a hot pan with some oil—but do it wrong and you've got either an overcooked hockey puck or a mushy mouthful of raw seafood. The trick, according to Jamie, is to keep the scallops just raw in the center.

1. Let the scallops come to room temperature, about 10 minutes.

2. Pat them dry with paper towels and season with salt.

3. Heat canola or grapeseed oil in a 10- to 12-inch stainless-steel pan over medium-high heat.

4. When you see ribbons in the oil, add a few scallops to the pan.

5. Reduce the heat to medium and cook until the outside of the scallops just starts to brown, about 1½ minutes.

6. Flip them over and turn off the heat (but keep them on the stove).

7. Add 1 tablespoon unsalted butter and baste with a spoon for about 30 seconds.

8. Serve right away.

> "People always overcook scallops. They should not be rubbery or chewy!"

FOOD PHILOSOPHY: I use the best possible ingredients, mostly local and sustainable.

INSPIRATION FOR RECIPES: I generally get a farm list of produce and work outward from there, formulating my recipes based on what's in season.

GO-TO INGREDIENTS: Bacon and butter.

FAVORITE BITE: Heirloom tomato salad with avocado and onion.

FAVORITE SCALLOP DISHES: Served raw, with sea salt, kaffir lime oil, pickled jalapeños, crispy shallots, and micro cilantro. Scallop and clam chowder with smoked bacon and potatoes.

JAMIE'S SEARED SCALLOPS WITH FENNEL CREAM

WINNER!

FENNEL PURÉE

3 fennel bulbs, trimmed, cored, and chopped, fronds reserved for garnish

¼ cup olive oil

Salt

8 cloves garlic, roasted

¼ cup crème fraîche

¾ to 1½ cups chicken stock, low-sodium broth, or water

FENNEL SALAD

2 fennel bulbs, trimmed and cored, fronds reserved for garnish

20 fresh mint leaves, cut into chiffonade

2 oranges, supremed and chopped

½ cup pitted green olives, thinly sliced

Juice of 1 orange

2 tablespoons lemon oil

Salt

SEA SCALLOPS

16 large sea scallops (about 1 pound)

Salt and freshly ground pepper

1 tablespoon olive oil

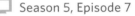

2 tablespoons lemon oil

SERVES 4

FOR THE FENNEL PURÉE: Preheat the oven to 375°F.

Put the fennel in a roasting pan and drizzle with the olive oil and salt to taste. Cover the pan with aluminum foil and roast until soft, about 1 hour. Transfer the cooked fennel to a food processor and process until smooth. Add the roasted garlic and crème fraîche and process the mixture again until smooth. Taste and adjust the seasoning. Pass the purée through a sieve to ensure a smooth consistency, adding stock as needed. Set aside and keep warm.

FOR THE FENNEL SALAD: With a mandoline, thinly slice the fennel bulbs and put the slices in a medium bowl. Add the mint, orange supremes, and olives. Mix in the orange juice and lemon oil, season to taste with salt, and set aside.

FOR THE SCALLOPS: Remove the tough muscle from the side of each scallop, if necessary. Pat the scallops dry and season with salt and pepper. In a medium sauté pan or skillet, heat the olive oil over medium-high heat, then sear the scallops until golden brown and just opaque, 1 to 2 minutes on each side.

To serve, place a portion of the fennel purée in the center of each plate. Top each with 4 scallops. Top the scallops with a serving of the fennel salad. Drizzle with the lemon oil and garnish with the reserved fennel fronds.

Prep time: 1 hour, 30 minutes

Season 5, Episode 7

Elimination Challenge: Cook a dish that expresses your individuality.

HUNG'S SASHIMI DEMO

Hung Huynh was born with a cleaver in his hand, having grown up in his parents' restaurant, and he chopped and sliced his way through the competition. At the Season 3 finale, he blew away the judges with his Hamachi with Pea Shoots (facing page) and won the Top Chef title.

"I am trained in French techniques, but I am strongly rooted in Asian flavors because that's what I grew up with."

ON CULINARY INFLUENCES: I am very influenced by my mother's cooking. Also, I am always reading, researching, talking to chefs—I'm always curious about the way things are done.

GO-TO INGREDIENT: Fish sauce.

FAVORITE KNIFE: I use one knife for everything: A 10½-inch Misono UX 10 slicer.

BALANCE: Chefs are always thinking about balance. Does it need more acid? What kind? Citrus? You develop flavor in that way.

HOW TO PREPARE SASHIMI

Here are Hung's tips on making sashimi at home.

1. You can't just make any fish into sashimi. You want a small saltwater fish that swims fast. Not monkfish or catfish; there is too much potential for bacteria.

2. When buying fish, check that it has a natural clear slime and does not smell fishy.

3. Check the eyes: they should be clear, not cloudy. Check the gills: they should be dark red, not brown.

4. Have the fish gutted and scaled for you.

5. At home, rinse the fish well under cold running water and pat it dry.

6. Fillet the fish (see page 104).

7. Trim away the ragged flesh around the belly part (stomach lining) and rinse the fillet one more time in cold, lightly salted fresh water.

8. Skin the fillet.

9. Slice the fillet crosswise to the desired thickness.

Hung's Favorite Ways to Serve Sashimi

- Mix soy sauce with citrus juice such as lime, grapefruit, or orange, and serve this dipping sauce with the fresh fish.

- Mix wasabi with water to make a paste, and serve with fish and pickled ginger.

- Serve sashimi with a sprinkling of sea salt, good olive oil, freshly chopped herbs, and fresh lemon juice.

HUNG'S HAMACHI WITH PEA SHOOTS

FINGERLING POTATO CHIPS

8 ounces fingerling potatoes
(about 4 potatoes)

Canola oil for deep-frying

Salt and freshly ground pepper

PEA-SHOOT SALAD

2 handfuls pea shoots, spun dry

1 teaspoon olive oil

Juice of 1/2 lemon, or as needed

Salt and freshly ground pepper

4 to 6 ounces sashimi-grade *hamachi*
(yellowtail) fillet, thinly sliced

Tomato Vinaigrette (below)
for serving

SERVES 2

FOR THE FINGERLING POTATO CHIPS: With a mandoline, slice the potatoes so thinly they are transparent, about 1/16 inch thick. Pour 2 inches of oil into a large, heavy skillet and heat over medium-high heat to 300°F on a deep-frying thermometer. Line a baking sheet with paper towels. Add the potato slices, working in batches to avoid crowding, and fry until crisp and golden brown, 3 to 5 minutes. Remove the chips from the oil with a slotted spoon and transfer to the paper towels to drain. Season with salt and pepper. Set aside.

FOR THE PEA-SHOOT SALAD: Dress the pea shoots with the olive oil and with lemon juice to taste. Season with salt and pepper.

To serve, divide the *hamachi* slices among 2 salad plates. Top with the pea-shoot salad, dividing evenly, and drizzle the plate with the vinaigrette. Garnish with the potato chips.

Prep time: 30 minutes

Season 3, Episode 15

Elimination Challenge:
Prepare a three-course meal to be served to a table of culinary luminaries.

HOW TO MAKE

tomato vinaigrette

1 cup yellow cherry tomatoes

3 tablespoons extra-virgin olive oil

2 tablespoons sherry vinegar

1/2 teaspoon prepared mustard

1/2 teaspoon sugar

Salt and freshly ground pepper

Combine the tomatoes, oil, vinegar, mustard, and sugar in a blender and blend until smooth. Season to taste with salt and pepper.

"This dish is a play on fish and chips. The flavors are clean and fresh, and the fingerling potato chips add crunch."

HUNG, SEASON 3 WINNER

LEAH'S FARROTTO
WITH RED SNAPPER AND PORCINIS

SAUCE AND *FARROTTO*

1 pound *guanciale*, pancetta, or bacon, chopped

1 pound small or medium shrimp, in the shell

1½ onions, cut into small dice

1½ fennel bulbs, trimmed, cored, and cut into small dice

3 cloves garlic, minced

2 *peperoncini* peppers, minced

2 tablespoons tomato paste

2/3 cup dry white wine

Two 28-ounce cans whole peeled tomatoes

3½ cups water

Salt and freshly ground pepper

1½ cups fish stock

1 cup *farro*

¼ cup chopped fresh mint

¼ cup chopped fresh oregano

....

MUSHROOMS

1 tablespoon olive oil

4 ounces dried cepe or porcini mushrooms, reconstituted in warm water and drained, or 8 ounces fresh porcinis, cleaned and trimmed

Salt and freshly ground pepper

RED SNAPPER

1 tablespoon grapeseed or vegetable oil

4 red snapper fillets, about 6 ounces each, skin on

Salt and freshly ground pepper

Prep time: 2 hours

Season 5, Episode 1

Elimination Challenge:
Create a dish that represents the ethnic cuisine of a New York neighborhood.

SERVES 4

FOR THE SAUCE AND *FARROTTO*: Line 2 baking sheets with paper towels. In a large, heavy-bottomed saucepan, cook ½ pound of the *guanciale* over medium-high heat until the fat is rendered. Transfer the *guanciale* to the paper towels, leaving the fat in the pan. Add the shrimp and sauté in the fat until pink and slightly toasted, 2 minutes. Remove the shrimp with a slotted spoon and place on the paper towels. Add half of the onions to the pan and cook until translucent, 10 minutes. Stir in half of the fennel and cook until soft and translucent, 8 to 10 minutes. Add half of the garlic and all of the *peperoncini* and sauté for 2 minutes. Add the tomato paste and brown with the other ingredients. Stir in ⅓ cup of the wine and scrape up any browned bits from the bottom of the pan. Add the whole peeled tomatoes and 2 cups of the water and bring to a simmer.

Peel and devein the cooked shrimp and coarsely chop. Add the shrimp meat to the sauce and season with salt and pepper. Continue to simmer until the sauce thickens and the flavors meld, about 20 minutes.

In a saucepan, combine the fish stock and the remaining 1½ cups water over medium-low heat and bring to a gentle simmer.

Meanwhile, in a large, heavy pot over medium-high heat, cook the remaining ½ pound *guanciale* until the fat is rendered. Add the remaining onions and fennel and cook until tender, about 10 minutes. Add the remaining garlic and the *farro*. Stir until the *farro* is lightly toasted. Pour in the remaining ⅓ cup wine and cook until it evaporates. Add ½ cup of the warm stock mixture and cook, stirring, until absorbed. Continue adding the liquid, ½ cup at a time, stirring after each addition until fully absorbed. Cook until the *farro* is tender but firm to the bite, 20 to 25 minutes. Stir in the mint and oregano, season with salt and pepper, and set aside.

FOR THE MUSHROOMS: In a medium sauté pan, heat the olive oil over medium-high heat. Add the mushrooms and sauté until golden brown. Season with salt and pepper.

FOR THE RED SNAPPER: In a large, heavy-bottomed sauté pan or skillet, heat the grapeseed oil over high heat until it is almost smoking. Season the fillets with salt and pepper. Sear the snapper skin-side down, then lower the heat to medium and cook for 4 minutes, pressing frequently with a spatula to keep the fillets flat. Turn the fish over and cook for an additional 2 minutes. Transfer to a plate.

To serve, mound a serving of the *farrotto* in the center of each plate. Place a snapper fillet on top of the *farrotto*. Spoon the sauce around the plate and on the fish. Garnish with a spoonful of the mushrooms.

"I definitely know Italian cuisine. I worked in Italy, I lived there, and the restaurant I work in now is Italian."

LEAH, SEASON 5

ABOUT AN INGREDIENT

farro

Legend has it that boiled *farro* sustained Julius Caesar's army as they conquered the rest of Europe. It's not so unrealistic when you consider that this hearty whole grain, which is grown mainly in central Italy, is extremely high in protein and is said to protect the body against heart attacks and other maladies. It also tastes good, especially when cooked in chicken or vegetable broth to make a *farro* risotto, or *farrotto*.

FILLET-O-FISH

Cutting a whole fish into user-friendly fillets can be pretty intimidating. Even many of the chef'testants were nervous when tasked with cutting up monkfish in the Mise-en-Place Relays or sardines in the Eric Ripert Fish Fillet Quickfire Challenge of Season 5. Here are general instructions for filleting a whole fish. Note that some flat fish, such as sole, are more difficult to fillet and best left to your fishmonger.

With kitchen shears, trim the fins from the sides, top, and back of the fish.

Using a thin, sharp boning knife, make a diagonal cut behind the gills from the top of the head to the belly, to separate the body from the head.

Make a long cut just above the spine, from the head to the tail.

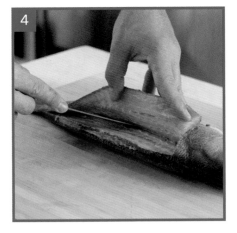

Going back to the head side, slide the knife against the backbone using swift, clean cuts to separate the flesh from the backbone, lifting the fillet with the other hand as you cut.

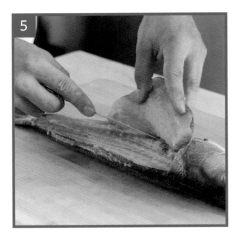

Remove the first fillet. Turn the fish over and repeat steps 2 through 4 to free the second fillet.

If you wish to remove the skin, place the fillet skin-side down and tail end toward you on the cutting board. Slide your knife under the flesh, angling it downward, and hold down the skin with the fingers of your other hand as you carefully cut away from you, separating the flesh from the skin.

HOSEA'S FISH-ROASTING DEMO

As executive chef at Jax Fish House in Boulder, Colorado, Hosea Rosenberg, winner of *Top Chef* Season 5, knows just about everything there is to know about cooking fish.

HOW TO ROAST FISH

Learning to fillet fish is a useful technique for any cook, but real seafood chefs love to cook fish whole and unadulterated. It's easy to cook and impressive to serve, fish eyes and all.

1. Start with a fresh whole fish that has been gutted and scaled. Preheat the oven to 425°F.

2. Stuff the cavity with fresh herbs and lemon. Sprinkle with sea salt and cracked pepper all over, inside and out.

3. Make 3 parallel slices to score the skin on both sides of the fish. Put the fish in an oval copper-bottom or heavy-duty roasting pan.

4. Drizzle olive oil into the pan, and scatter in whole garlic cloves. Warm briefly on the stove top.

5. Roast the fish, covered; timing will depend on the size and type of fish, but as a rule of thumb, about 12 minutes per pound.

6. Drizzle the fish with lemon juice and olive oil and present it whole. Serve the fish right from the pan or a platter at the table, family style.

Hosea's Favorite Ways to Prepare Fish:

- Searing ahi.
- Grilling marlin or other meaty fish.
- Broiling cod or other white fish.
- Roasting whole bass or snapper.
- Poaching halibut.
- Curing sable fish or salmon.
- Smoking salmon.

"I didn't go to school, and because of that, I don't know the French word for a single damn thing."

HIS SIGNATURE STYLE: Flavor is paramount, more than anything else. My food is very approachable, simple yet refined. It just needs to taste good.

ON FAUX CAVIAR: I'm tired of faux caviar. Okay, there are these little beads of balsamic, but they are not always that fun to eat.

MOTTO: When in doubt, add butter.

LIFE AFTER *TOP CHEF*: Life has definitely changed. I'll be at the airport and get a small crowd around me; people want to take their picture with me. The show really turns you into a bit of a celebrity.

HOSEA'S BACON-WRAPPED HALIBUT

HALIBUT

4 pieces Alaskan halibut, about 6 ounces each

4 slices thin-cut bacon

Salt and freshly ground pepper

Canola oil for frying

....

VEGETABLES

6 small Yukon gold potatoes, blanched and peeled

1 tablespoon olive oil

Salt and freshly ground pepper

2 tablespoons unsalted butter

2 small yellow beets, greens reserved, beets parboiled and peeled

16 haricots verts, blanched and shocked (see page 15)

2 shallots, sliced

4 cloves garlic, chopped

Leaves from 1 small bunch fresh flat-leaf parsley, chopped

BEURRE BLANC

1 cup dry white wine

1/4 cup fresh lemon juice

1 shallot, sliced

10 peppercorns

3 bay leaves

1/4 cup heavy cream

3/4 cup tablespoons (1 1/2 sticks) cold unsalted butter, cut into cubes

2 tablespoons whole-grain mustard

SERVES 4

FOR THE HALIBUT: Preheat the oven to 350°F. Wrap the bacon tightly around the halibut. Season with salt and pepper. In a large, ovenproof sauté pan or skillet, heat the oil over medium heat. Sear the halibut until brown. Transfer the pan to the oven and roast until the fish is just cooked through, about 2 minutes.

FOR THE VEGETABLES: Raise the oven temperature to 425°F. Slice the potatoes into rounds. Toss with the olive oil and season with salt and pepper, then roast until lightly browned, about 10 minutes. Remove from the oven and set aside.

Slice the beets into matchstick-sized pieces. Slice the beans into thirds. Chop the beet greens. In a large sauté pan, melt the butter over medium-high heat and sauté the shallots and garlic until soft but not brown, about 1 minute. Add the beets and beans to the pan with a little salt and pepper, raise the heat to high, and sauté, for about 2 minutes. Add the greens to the pan and take it off the heat. Continue stirring until the greens have wilted, about 2 minutes. Stir in the parsley. Set aside.

FOR THE BEURRE BLANC: In a medium saucepan over medium heat, combine the wine, lemon juice, shallot, peppercorns, and bay leaves and bring to a simmer. Reduce until syrupy. Add the cream and reduce until a thick sauce forms. Slowly whisk in the chilled butter cubes until completely emulsified. Strain through a fine-mesh sieve into a clean saucepan. Add the mustard and check the seasoning. Keep warm.

To serve, arrange the potato slices in a ring on each plate. Fill the ring with the other vegetables. Top with the fish. Spoon the sauce around the plate.

Prep time: Under 2 hours

Season 5, Episode 7

Elimination Challenge:
Cook a dish that expresses your individuality.

ABOUT A TECHNIQUE
barding and larding

Both barding and larding involve slipping some bacon into your otherwise lean meat or fish dish. The important difference is that with larding you use a special needle (called a larding needle) to insert little pieces of bacon into your meat that will melt during cooking. Barding, or wrapping food in bacon or other fat, requires no special tools.

KEVIN'S OIL-POACHED ARCTIC CHAR

PICKLED TURNIP SALSA VERDE

1 medium purple-top turnip, peeled and finely diced

1 shallot, finely diced

2 cups cider vinegar

1/2 cup firmly packed brown sugar

1 star anise pod

1 cinnamon stick

1 teaspoon peppercorns

Leaves from 1 bunch fresh flat-leaf parsley

Leaves from 3 fresh tarragon sprigs

Leaves from 1 bunch fresh basil

1/2 bunch fresh chives

1/4 cup extra-virgin olive oil

1/3 cup canola oil, plus 1 tablespoon

Orange oil or grated orange zest

Salt

1 English cucumber

1/2 fennel bulb, trimmed, cored, and finely diced

3 ribs celery, finely diced

Freshly ground pepper

....

BRAISED ROMAINE

1 English cucumber, peeled and cut into chunks

1/4 cup water

4 tablespoons unsalted butter, cut into pieces

1 head romaine lettuce, inner leaves only

Salt and freshly ground pepper

....

ARCTIC CHAR

1 cup extra-virgin olive oil

3 sprigs fresh thyme

6 cloves garlic, smashed

2 Arctic char, salmon, or sea trout fillets, 6 to 8 ounces each

Salt

Fennel pollen or ground fennel seeds for dusting

SERVES 4

FOR THE PICKLED TURNIP SALSA VERDE: Combine the turnip and shallot in a large, shallow, heatproof bowl.

In a small saucepan, combine the vinegar, brown sugar, star anise, cinnamon stick, and peppercorns and bring to a rolling boil over high heat. Pour the mixture over the turnip mixture and let cool to room temperature.

Bring a pot of water to a boil and have a bowl of ice water ready. Blanch the parsley, tarragon, basil, and chives, drain, and shock the herbs in the ice bath (see page 15) before draining again. Transfer to a blender with the olive oil and 1/3 cup canola oil and blend until smooth. Mix in the orange oil. Season with salt to taste. Set aside.

Finely dice half of the cucumber. Reserve the remaining half. Add the diced cucumber and fennel to the turnip mixture and drain. Remove the cinnamon stick and star anise.

Place a medium sauté pan over high heat until smoking. Add the remaining 1 table-spoon canola oil and sauté the celery until caramelized but still crisp, about 4 min-utes. Add the cooked celery to the pickled vegetables and toss with just enough herb

CONTINUED

⏱ Prep time: 1 hour, 30 minutes

🖥 Season 6, Episode 1

🔪 Elimination Challenge: Cook a dish based on one of your personal vices.

KEVIN DISHES

"I decided that sloth is a vice I could embody. I often fall victim to misjudging my time and to waiting forever to do something that should have been done more urgently. By slowing down something urgent (the cooking time for fish) and by speeding up something that is normally accomplished in due time (the cooking of turnips), I would hopefully find a natural balance for my own shortcomings."

purée to coat the vegetables, about 6 tablespoons. Taste and adjust the seasoning with salt and pepper. Set the salsa verde aside, and reserve the remaining herb purée.

FOR THE BRAISED ROMAINE: In a blender or food processor, purée the cucumber, adding a few tablespoons water, if necessary. Transfer the purée onto a square of cheesecloth set over a small bowl and squeeze the cucumber liquid into the bowl. Be sure to squeeze out all the liquid. Discard the solids.

In a large sauté pan, bring the water to a boil over medium-high heat, and whisk in the butter a few pieces at a time until the completely emulsified. Mix the cucumber juice into the emulsion. Add the romaine leaves to the pan, reduce the heat to medium, and cook in the hot emulsion just until limp. Drain and season the leaves with salt and pepper. Keep warm.

FOR THE ARCTIC CHAR: Preheat the oven to 275°F.

In a sauté pan, heat the olive oil over medium-low heat. Add the thyme sprigs and garlic, remove from the heat, and let steep for 30 minutes. Strain into a large baking dish.

Season the fish fillets with salt and fennel pollen and place them in the baking dish with the oil. Bake, spooning the oil over fish several times, until opaque, 20 to 25 minutes.

To serve, streak a little herb purée on each plate. With a Microplane, grate a small amount of the reserved cucumber half over the romaine leaves. Place the romaine leaves on top of the herb purée and place a fish fillet on the romaine. Top with a little salsa verde and drizzle the plate with braising liquid.

NILS NOREN'S SALMON WITH NAPA CABBAGE AND CHORIZO

½ head napa cabbage

½ cup rice vinegar

2 tablespoons sugar

1 side wild salmon, about 4 pounds

Activa TG-RM transglutaminase (meat glue)

2 heads broccoli

6 cups milk

Salt and freshly ground pepper

Ground fennel seeds

One 750-ml bottle Madeira wine

4 cups veal stock

2 pieces Spanish chorizo, about 4 ounces, diced

Extra-virgin olive oil for drizzling

SERVES 6 TO 8

Core and cut the cabbage lengthwise into 3-inch thick slices. Place in a large bowl and add the vinegar and sugar. Place a weight on top of the cabbage and refrigerate overnight. Return the cabbage to room temperature when ready to continue.

Cut the salmon lengthwise into 4 strips. Sprinkle the salmon strips with the transglutaminase, then roll into cylinders. Refrigerate.

Have ready a bowl of ice water. Cut the broccoli florets into small pieces and finely slice the broccoli stems. In a medium saucepan, bring the milk to a boil and add the broccoli florets. Cook until soft, 5 to 7 minutes. With a slotted spoon, remove the florets from the hot milk and transfer them to a blender. Process until completely puréed. Transfer the purée to a bowl and nestle in the ice bath to cool. Bring the milk to a boil again and repeat the same procedure with the broccoli stems. Discard the milk. Mix the two purées and season with salt, pepper, and ground fennel seeds.

In a medium saucepan, simmer the Madeira and veal stock over medium-high heat until reduced by four-fifths, about 1 hour. Remove from the heat and set aside.

In a medium sauté pan or skillet, cook the chorizo over medium-high heat, stirring occasionally, until browned, about 3 minutes. Remove from the heat. Drain the marinated cabbage and stir it into the chorizo. Set aside.

Cut the salmon cylinders horizontally into ½-inch portions. Drizzle a rimmed baking sheet with olive oil and put the salmon on the sheet. Season with salt and pepper. Place a large, shallow pan of water over two burners and bring to a simmer over medium heat. Place the pan of salmon on top of the hot-water bath and cook until the salmon reaches the desired doneness, 5 to 7 minutes.

To serve, mound the cabbage mixture in the center of each plate. Place the salmon on top and spoon the broccoli purée around the plate. Sauce with the Madeira reduction.

🕐 **Prep time:** 2 hours, 30 minutes, plus overnight for cabbage

🖥 *Top Chef Masters*, Season 1, Episode 5

🔪 **Elimination Challenge:** Create a mini appetizer, entrée, and dessert for 100 people.

ABOUT AN INGREDIENT

meat glue

The latest trick in the molecular gastronomy pantry, meat glue (transglutaminase, sold under the brand name Activa) is a chemical compound that helps bind proteins together. In this recipe, Nils Noren uses the Activa to keep his salmon cylinders tightly rolled. In Season 6, Bryan used Activa to great effect to "glue" together two skin-side-out pieces of halibut in the French Classics Elimination.

CHEF BIOS: SEASON 6

FOR SEASONS 1 TO 5, CHECK OUT *TOP CHEF: THE COOKBOOK* AND *TOP CHEF: THE QUICKFIRE COOKBOOK*.

MICHAEL VOLTAGGIO

HOMETOWN: Frederick, MD
FUN FACT: Has shared a kitchen with TC alums Marcel, Ilan, and Hung
CURRENTLY: Chef de Cuisine at The Dining Room, Langham Huntington Hotel, L.A.

Michael is a force to be reckoned with. The first chef'testant to have earned a Michelin Star, Michael was as comfortable using liquid nitrogen in mind-bending molecular dishes, as he was creating traditional fare with genuine flavor and harmony. He edged out his brother for the Top Chef title.

WINNER!

BRYAN VOLTAGGIO

HOMETOWN: Frederick, MD
FUN FACT: Is now proud owner of a vintage Corvette
CURRENTLY: Chef-Owner of VOLT, in Frederick, MD

Bryan graduated from the Culinary Institute of America and was a protégé of Charlie Palmer before opening his own restaurant; it was Bryan that inspired his little brother to enter the profession. A real perfectionist in the kitchen, Bryan was confident and consistent all season long, making it to the finals in Napa.

KEVIN GILLESPIE

HOMETOWN: Small town outside Atlanta, GA
FUN FACT: Once worked with Richard B. at Two Urban Licks
CURRENTLY: Chef-owner of Woodfire Grill in Atlanta

From escargots with bacon jam to hearty kale with mushrooms (see page 26), Kevin wowed everyone with his upscale Southern comfort food. Pure skill earned him a spot in the finals, where he battled the mighty Voltaggio brothers; being an all around good guy and a team player snagged him the title of Fan Favorite.

JENNIFER CARROLL

HOMETOWN: Philadelphia, PA
FUN FACT: Can eat her own weight in junk food
CURRENTLY: Executive Chef at Ten Arts, by Eric Ripert

Jennifer claims to have made men cry in the kitchen, and it's not hard to believe—this uber-talented chef showed her toughness in winning several challenges. In an up-and-down season, she nearly got the ax for a weak vegetarian dish for Natalie Portman. But she finished strong, and gave her mentor, Chef Eric Ripert, reason to be proud.

ELI KIRSHTEIN

HOMETOWN: Atlanta, GA
FUN FACT: No longer lives with his parents
CURRENTLY: Left Atlanta to be Executive Chef at Solo in NYC

This boy wonder has achieved a lot in his short years, working with such luminary chefs as Kevin Rathbun and Richard B. In the middle of the pack much of the season, he finished strong by winning the Snack Food Quickfire, and satisfying both Padma and Nigella Lawson with a hearty breakfast in bed.

ROBIN LEVENTHAL

HOMETOWN: Sun Valley, ID
FUN FACT: Pursued an MFA in ceramics
CURRENTLY: Executive Chef, See Sound Lounge, Seattle

A cancer survivor with a strong personality, Robin alienated nearly everyone on the show. Robin won the Angel/Devil Quickfire with her Apple Crisp and Fruit Mêlée (page 192), and garnered kudos for her dessert during Restaurant Wars.

MIKE ISABELLA

HOMETOWN: Little Ferry, NJ
FUN FACT: Favorite dish is octopus
CURRENTLY: Executive Chef, Zaytinya

Never afraid to speak his mind, Mike showed both talent and abrasiveness. He got in trouble with a few under-seasoned dishes, but won the tough Cactus Quickfire Challenge. He was eventually let go for a failed leek dish made for Natalie Portman.

LAURINE WICKETT

HOMETOWN: Rochester, NY
FUN FACT: Bonded with fellow San Franciscans Preeti and Mattin
CURRENTLY: Chef-Owner of Left Coast Catering, San Francisco

Laurine may not have made it to the finale in Napa, but anyone who serves Bacon Doughnuts (page 207) in the first episode is a Top Chef in our book. This earthy San Franciscan rode out some tough challenges in Season 6.

ASH FULK

HOMETOWN: Pleasant Hill, CA
FUN FACT: Felt he had bad chemistry with Padma
CURRENTLY: Sous-chef at Trestle on Tenth, NYC

The only New York–based chef on Season 6, Ash garnered kudos for his Chocolate–Peanut Butter Bread Pudding (see page 199). The judges declared his cold sliced pork loin to be lacking in flavor.

ASHLEY MERRIMAN

HOMETOWN: Center Sandwich, NH
FUN FACT: Bonded with Ash
CURRENTLY: Executive Chef, Branzino, Seattle

Ashley has worked in top kitchens on both coasts and picked up a good many tattoos along the way. A graduate of the ICE in New York, Ashley exuded confidence and calm.

RON DUPRAT

HOMETOWN: Mare Rouge, Haiti
FUN FACT: Won Montauk Chowder Competition three years in a row
CURRENTLY: Consulting, making appearances, working on a book

Survivor of a harrowing trip at sea from Haiti, Ron has been acclaimed as executive chef at Noble House and Pelican Bay in Naples, Florida, and at the Montauk Yacht Club in Montauk, New York.

MATTIN NOBLIA

HOMETOWN: Biarritz, France
FUN FACT: Loves Jessica Alba
CURRENTLY: Chef-Owner, Iluna Basque in San Francisco

Mattin successfully opened his own restaurant at a very young age. He scored high on the Cactus Quickfire but was sent home in the same episode for serving badly executed ceviche to ranch hands in the scorching desert.

HECTOR SANTIAGO

HOMETOWN: San Juan, Puerto Rico
FUN FACT: Obsessed with hot peppers
CURRENTLY: Chef-Owner of Pura Vida, Atlanta

From the outset, Hector claimed he cooked with *cojones*—he proved it by serving a deep-fried prime steak to Wolfgang Puck in episode 1. He impressed the judges with his Tofu Ceviche (page 128), and is lighting up the vibrant food scene in Atlanta.

JESSE SANDLIN

HOMETOWN: Baltimore, MD
FUN FACT: Always has bacon, butter, duck fat, and cumin on hand
CURRENTLY: Executive Chef, Abacrombie Fine Foods

Though strong and experienced, self-taught Jesse never quite got her footing. She was sent home after an elimination Quickfire, in which the three bottom candidates had 20 minutes to whip up an *amuse-bouche*.

PREETI MISTRY

HOMETOWN: San Francisco, CA
FUN FACT: Born in London, England
CURRENTLY: Bon Appétit Management Company, San Francisco

Despite her Cordon Bleu education, Preeti seemed lost among the high-rolling chefs of Season 6. She was sent home after the Thunderbirds Challenge for too ardently defending a mediocre pasta salad before the judges.

EVE ARONOFF

HOMETOWN: Ann Arbor, MI
FUN FACT: Published a cookbook,
CURRENTLY: Chef-Owner of Eve in Ann Arbor

Educated at the Cordon Bleu in Paris, Eve Aronoff brought impressive credentials to the show. But her cooking style seemed out of step with the judges' tastes.

JENNIFER ZAVALA

HOMETOWN: Cromwell, CT
FUN FACT: Comes from an Italian and Mexican background
CURRENTLY: Sous Chef at Xochitl in Philadelphia

Jen made a strong impression with her extensive body art but was sent home after serving a chile relleno stuffed with seitan.

FOREIGN EXCHANGE: COOKING WITH GLOBAL FLAVORS

133

121

139

125

145

GOING GLOBAL

With so many talented young chefs of such different origins gathered together, it's not surprising that *Top Chef* has become a kind of platform for showcasing interesting and exciting ingredients from around the world. These chefs have given us the confidence to add some new tastes to our cooking, to go outside our usual comfort zone and experiment with flavor profiles like Southeast Asian, Indian, North African, Mexican, and Japanese, to name a few. Below is a very brief introduction to some of the ingredients featured in these cuisines.

NORTH AFRICAN

1. **RAS EL HANOUT:** This Moroccan spice mix can contain up to thirty ingredients. The broad outline consists of ginger, coriander, cumin, salt, pepper, and turmeric. In Season 6, Eli turned out a tasty dish of Mussels with Ras el Hanout and Sherry Caramel, and Richard B. smoked it for his Smoked Crab Cakes (page 162).

2. **HARISSA:** This thick, spicy sauce is made up primarily of red chiles, garlic, and olive oil, combined with spices such as coriander and cumin. In Season 6, Mike I. got kudos for his Oil-Poached Halibut on Top of Eggplant Purée spiced with green-olive *harissa*.

MEXICAN

3. **CHAYOTE:** This green squash is used widely in Mexican and Central American cooking. You can shave it into a salad, roast it, stuff it, and do just about anything to it. In Season 4, Antonia pickled it along with papaya and sweet peppers for her Honey Pork Belly at the finale in Puerto Rico.

4. **DRIED CHILES:** If you want to attempt the *mole negro* that helped win Rick Bayless the title of Top Chef Master or Kevin's winning version of the dish (see page 140) in Season 6, get ready to know your dried chiles:

ANCHO: Mild, dried poblano pepper
PASILLA: Medium-mild dried *chilaca* pepper
GUAJILLO: Medium-hot dried chile with a thick skin
MORITA: Similar to chipotle; a smoked, dried red jalapeño

INDIAN

5. **TAMARIND:** Also popular in Mexican and Southeast Asian cuisines, sweet-tart tamarind is a key ingredient in many Indian chutneys. Hubert Keller used tamarind concentrate in his Vietnamese Gazpacho on *Top Chef Masters* Season 1.

6. **GARAM MASALA:** This spice mix is essential to Indian cooking; it adds depth of flavor to all kinds of curries, spice rubs, and sauces. The mix usually includes coriander, cumin, pepper, ginger, and cardamom.

JAPANESE

7. **SHISO:** Similar to mint, this green leafy herb is used as an accent and garnish in many dishes, in Japanese and other Asian cuisines. In Season 5, Carla used the herb in her pan-global Crab-Shiso Soup (page 121) at the finale in New Orleans.

8. **YUZU:** A citrus fruit with a tart flavor, *yuzu* is an integral ingredient in *ponzu* sauce and many other preparations, and adds a bit of Asian flair to a *gastrique* or sauce. It's been used many times on *Top Chef*, from Andrew's Squid Ceviche (page 167) to Rick Moonen's Opakapaka and Barramundi Ceviche on *Top Chef Masters*.

SOUTHEAST ASIAN

9. **KAFFIR LIME LEAVES:** These leaves add a lusty, citrusy taste to all kinds of Thai curries, and to Indonesian and Malaysian dishes as well. Wylie Dufresne cooked lime leaves with Dr Pepper to make a syrup to top his grilled cheese sandwich on *Top Chef Masters* Season 1.

10. **GALANGAL:** Used by Lee Anne to flavor her Chicken in Red Curry Sauce in Season 1, this gingerlike rhizome lends a sweet, aromatic edge to curries and soups.

CARLA'S CRAB-SHISO SOUP

COURT BOUILLON

6 cups cold water

1/4 cup white wine vinegar

1 carrot, peeled and cut into rondelles

1 rib celery, cut into 1-inch segments

1 onion, coarsely chopped

1 sprig fresh thyme

2 bay leaves

10 sprigs fresh flat-leaf parsley

1 1/2 teaspoons sea salt

1 teaspoon peppercorns

6 fresh blue crabs or 8 ounces jumbo lump crabmeat, picked through for shell bits

CHAYOTE-THAI BASIL RELISH

1 chayote squash, seeded, peeled, and finely diced

1/4 cup finely diced red bell pepper

2 tablespoons fresh Thai basil leaves, cut into chiffonade

Grated zest and juice of 1 lime

2 tablespoons minced lemongrass

2 teaspoons peeled and grated fresh ginger

1 habanero chile, seeded and minced

2 tablespoons rice vinegar

1/4 cup extra-virgin olive oil

Salt and freshly ground pepper

CHILLED SHISO SOUP

1 cup chopped *shiso* (perilla) leaves

1 cup baby spinach leaves

2 teaspoons peeled and minced fresh ginger

1 clove garlic, minced

1 small onion, finely chopped

2 tablespoons mirin

2 tablespoons rice vinegar

1 cup dry white wine

Juice of 2 limes

1/2 teaspoon salt

1 cup crème fraîche or sour cream

SERVES 4

FOR THE COURT BOUILLON: Combine all the ingredients in a large stockpot over medium-high heat. Bring to a rolling boil and boil for 15 minutes. Remove from the heat and let cool, then strain.

If using live blue crabs, boil the court bouillon as directed, then drop in the crabs and boil until the shells turn reddish, about 6 minutes. Remove the crabs from the pot, let cool, and reserve the court bouillon. Crack the shells, pick the crab meat (which should be opaque white), and chill in the refrigerator.

FOR THE CHAYOTE-THAI BASIL RELISH: Combine all the ingredients in a medium bowl. Taste and adjust the seasoning with salt, pepper, and habanero. Set aside.

FOR THE CHILLED SHISO SOUP: In a blender or food processor, combine the *shiso*, spinach, ginger, garlic, onion, mirin, vinegar, wine, lime juice, and salt. Add the reserved court bouillon and blend, adding water in 1/2 cup increments as needed to achieve the desired consistency. On low speed, blend in the crème fraîche. Taste and adjust the seasoning.

To serve, spoon the soup into serving bowls and top with the relish and crabmeat.

Prep time: 1 hour, 30 minutes

Season 5, Episode 14

Elimination Challenge:
Cook the best three-course meal of your life.

ABOUT AN INGREDIENT

court bouillon

Instead of a classic stock for this soup, Carla uses a court bouillon, which is a quick stock made with some acid (lemon or vinegar), herbs, and pepper. It's traditionally used for poaching fish or other delicate items, but can be used for anything: Ludo Lefebvre even used it to poach his pig's ear on *Top Chef Masters*.

Q + A

WITH

rick bayless

Through his acclaimed restaurants in Chicago, his television series, and many cookbooks, award-winning Chef Rick Bayless has introduced America to flavorful, authentic, high-end Mexican cuisine. He served as a guest judge on Season 4 in Chicago, where his restaurants Frontera Grill, Topolobampo, and Xoco can be found. He returned to compete on *Top Chef Masters*, where his consistently calm demeanor and impressive dishes, including a gourmet guacamole bar and a deeply complex *mole negro*, blew the judges away and led him to victory.

What was it like competing on *Top Chef Masters*?

It was the hardest experience of my whole life. I would even say that it's harder than opening a restaurant, which anyone will tell you is one of the hardest things in the world to do. If the challenge was something that would normally take three hours, they'd give us two hours.

What do you think about how you were portrayed on the show?

You get to see a different side of me than what you see in my own show. On my show I'm presenting things I am very excited about, and here I was working outside my comfort zone, in a competitive context. What you also see on *Top Chef Masters* is that the top chefs in the United States are really generous and nice people. I think hardly anyone expected that. The show proved that you don't have to yell and scream and be Gordon Ramsey to get to the top.

How excited were you to win?

We were standing in front of the judges, and my heart was just racing. When the scores were announced, I was totally blown away. I couldn't believe it! What an incredible thing to think about, that this guy who was raised in a BBQ restaurant in Oklahoma City would rise to the position of Top Chef Master.

What do you think put you over the top?

I just make food that lots of people like to eat. For the finale, I made all the dishes in a contemporary style, as if I were putting it on my menu today. I chose to do a reinterpretation as if it were going to be served at Topolobampo right now.

Did you taste the dishes made by your fellow Master chefs?

The food was astonishingly good. When you tasted the food, you really understood why these chefs were on *Top Chef Masters*. The regular chef'testants—the young people who are just getting started—they have a lot to learn, and it tastes like it.

What did you learn from cooking with these other Master chefs?

Because we were working under such time pressure, I didn't get a chance to watch what the others were doing nearly as much as I wanted to. But we would sit around the table in the green room and talk about what we had done and how we had done it. That part was just fantastic. The camaraderie in the kitchen was unbelievable. I've made friends that will now not just be professional acquaintances but lifelong friends.

You came across as very Zen. Are your kitchens as calm as you are?

What you saw is what you get. That's the way I am all the time. I'm fourth generation in a family of restaurant people. My parents taught me that when things fall apart, as the leader you need to stay calm, and then everyone else will too.

Do you cook a lot at home?

I cook for family and friends all the time at my house. On Monday afternoons I usually spend three hours making dinner, and we have friends over every Monday night. I have a wood-burning oven, so I cook a lot of stuff in there.

What's your favorite five-minute dish?

I would never make something that could be done that fast.

Do you think Mexican cuisine will receive more recognition due to your win?

For ages I have stood behind French and Italian cuisine and waited, waited for America to discover authentic, high-end, contemporary, wine-drinking (not just beer and margaritas!), flavorful Mexican food. I feel like I brought Mexican cuisine out and showed it to a different audience. We really opened people's eyes.

Do you have any food vices?

Besides doughnuts? I love really good doughnuts. At Xoco we make our own churros, so I've been eating a lot of those. For quality-control purposes, of course.

RICK BAYLESS'S VEGAN CORN TAMALE

CORN TAMALES

2 cups fresh corn kernels

1/2 cup vegetable shortening

2 tablespoons sugar

1/2 teaspoon salt

1/4 teaspoon baking powder

1 pound fresh *masa*

Eight 1-foot squares banana leaf, each run over a gas flame or broiled until softened

CHILE-BRAISED BEANS

1 pound dried black beans or three 15-ounce cans black beans

1 medium white onion, diced

Low-sodium chicken or vegetable broth or water, as needed

3 ancho chiles, seeded, toasted, and soaked

2 *pasilla de Oaxaca* chiles, toasted and soaked

4 cloves garlic, dry roasted in the peel, then peeled

Salt

1 large bunch *lacinato* (dinosaur) kale, stemmed and cut into 1-inch-wide slices (about 4 cups)

GLAZED MUSHROOMS AND BRAISED GREENS

2 tablespoons canola oil

4 large shiitake mushroom caps, brushed clean and cut into large cubes

3 to 4 tablespoons prepared chipotle salsa, blended smooth

1 tablespoon agave nectar

2 cups frisée

1 cup watercress, leaves and tender stems only

2 to 3 tablespoons fresh lime juice

Salt

SERVES 4

FOR THE CORN TAMALES: Put the corn in a food processor and process to a purée. Add the shortening, sugar, salt, and baking powder and process until smooth. Add the *masa* and blend until well incorporated.

Tear off 1 long, narrow strip from each banana-leaf square to use to tie the tamales, and set aside.

Divide the corn dough evenly among the banana squares, placing the portion in the center of each leaf. To wrap the tamales, bring the right and left sides of each leaf together and overlap them in the center. Then fold the bottom half of the leaf up to secure the dough. Loosely tie the tamale closed (leaving the top open) with a reserved banana-leaf strip.

Stand all the tamales upright in a vegetable steamer placed in a large, deep pot. Add about 1 inch of water to the pot and bring to a boil. Cover the pot tightly and steam the tamales for 1 hour, adding additional hot water to the pot as necessary. Remove the tamales from the steamer and set aside.

CONTINUED

🕐 Prep time: 2 hours, plus soaking beans

📺 *Top Chef Masters,* Season 1, Episode 8

🔪 Elimination Challenge: Create a vegan dish without gluten or soy.

ABOUT AN INGREDIENT

agave

Used to make tequila, the Mexican agave plant also produces a sweet syrup that is similar to honey. Vegans like it because no bees are exploited in the making of this sweetener. Chefs like it because it comes in different intensities, from light to caramel-colored, and it has a delicious, mild flavor.

FOR THE CHILE-BRAISED BEANS: If using dried beans, sort, rinse, and soak overnight in water to cover, then drain. Or, in a large pot, combine the beans with water to cover by 2 inches, bring to a boil, and cook for 2 minutes. Remove from the heat, cover, and let soak for 1 hour, then drain. Put the soaked beans in a large, heavy-bottomed pot over medium-high heat. Add the onion and broth to cover the beans. Bring to a boil, reduce the heat to achieve a gentle simmer, and cook until the beans are tender, 40 minutes to 1 hour.

If using canned beans, drain and rinse. Pour the beans with water to cover into a large, heavy-bottomed pot over medium-low heat. Add the onion and simmer until heated through and the onion is tender, 15 to 20 minutes.

When the beans are almost done, place the soaked chiles and the garlic in a blender or food processor and process until smooth. Press through a sieve into the pot of beans. Season to taste with salt. Add the kale and simmer until tender. Remove from the heat.

FOR THE GLAZED MUSHROOMS AND BRAISED GREENS: In a medium sauté pan, heat the oil over high heat. Add the shiitakes and sauté until brown. Add the salsa and agave nectar and reduce to a glaze, about 15 minutes. Toss in the frisée, watercress, and 2 tablespoons lime juice. Season with salt. Taste and adjust the seasoning with salt and additional lime juice, if needed.

To serve, spoon a portion of beans onto each plate and sprinkle with the mushrooms and greens. Place a tamale on top of the beans.

RICK BAYLESS'S CHIPS AND SALSA

SALSA MEXICANA

1 medium white onion, cut into medium dice

Hot green chiles to taste (usually 3 serranos or 2 small jalapeños), seeded, if desired, and minced

1¹/₂ pounds (about 3 medium-large round or 8 to 10 plum) ripe, red tomatoes, cut into medium dice

¹/₄ cup loosely packed chopped fresh cilantro

About ¹/₄ cup fresh lime juice

Salt

2 to 3 pounds large chips (preferably homemade or from a local tortilla factory) or small tostadas

1¹/₂ cups (about 6 ounces) Mexican *queso fresco* or *queso añejo* or other garnishing cheese like salted, pressed farmers cheese, firm goat cheese, mild feta, or pecorino romano, finely crumbled or grated

1¹/₂ cups (about 6 ounces) toasted pumpkin seeds

1¹/₂ cups sliced "nacho ring" pickled jalapeño chiles (you'll need an 11-ounce can)

1¹/₂ cups (about 4¹/₂ ounces) coarsely crumbled *chicharrones* (Mexican crisp-fried pork rind)

1 cup crumbled, crisp-fried bacon (4 to 5 medium-thick bacon slices)

Minced fresh herbs, such as chives, cilantro, epazote, or basil

Sliced scallions or pickled red onions

Roasted Garlic Guacamole (below)

SERVES 4 TO 10

FOR THE SALSA MEXICANA: Put the onion in a colander, rinse under cold tap water, shake off the excess, and transfer to a medium bowl. Add the green chiles, tomatoes, cilantro, and lime juice. Stir well, taste, and season with salt. Cover and refrigerate until serving.

To serve, garnish the chips as desired and accompany with the salsa.

> "We only had 30 minutes to come up with the entire menu and divide up the shopping list. At the buffet service, there was no water and no sanitation. It was a nightmare."
>
> RICK BAYLESS, *TOP CHEF MASTERS* SEASON 1 WINNER

Prep time: 20 minutes

Top Chef Masters, Season 1, Episode 9

Elimination Challenge: Create a buffet for 200 guests with a team of three sous-chefs.

HOW TO MAKE

roasted garlic guacamole

4 cloves garlic, unpeeled

4 ripe avocados, pitted, peeled, and chopped

¹/₄ cup loosely packed coarsely chopped fresh cilantro

2 tablespoons fresh lime juice, or as needed

Salt

In a dry skillet, roast the garlic over medium heat until blackened in spots, 10 to 15 minutes. Let cool, peel and chop. Mash together the garlic, avocados, cilantro, and lime juice. Season with salt. Cover with plastic wrap, pressing it directly on the surface of the guacamole. Refrigerate.

HECTOR'S TOFU CEVICHE

PICKLED GARLIC

1 tablespoon minced garlic

2 tablespoons rice vinegar

1/2 teaspoon salt

MANGO PEARLS

1 cup mango juice, well chilled

1 teaspoon agar-agar powder

4 cups canola oil, well chilled

CILANTRO-MINT PEARLS

1 cup cold water

1 teaspoon salt

Leaves from 1/2 bunch fresh cilantro

Leaves from 1/2 bunch fresh mint

Grated zest of 1/2 lime

1 teaspoon agar-agar powder

TOFU CEVICHE

1/2 cup fresh lemon juice

1/2 cup fresh lime juice

2 teaspoons kosher salt

2 tablespoons tequila

One 12-ounce package extra-firm tofu, drained and cubed

GARNISH

2 scallions

Ice water as needed

1 red bell pepper, seeded and cut into brunoise

1/2 cucumber, peeled, seeded, and cut into brunoise

Tortilla chips

🕐 **Prep time:** 1 hour, plus chilling

🖥 Season 6, Episode 2

🔪 Elimination Challenge:
Cater a bachelor/bachelorette party in two teams split by gender.

SERVES 4

FOR THE PICKLED GARLIC: In a saucepan of boiling salted water, blanch the garlic for 1 minute. Drain and place the garlic in a small ramekin. Add the vinegar and salt and cover the dish with plastic wrap. Set aside and let the garlic pickle for 30 minutes.

FOR THE MANGO PEARLS: In a medium saucepan, combine the mango juice and agar-agar and stir to combine well. Bring the mixture to a boil, stirring constantly, then reduce the heat and simmer until the agar-agar dissolves completely, about 2 minutes. Dispense the warm mango juice drop by drop into the cold canola oil to form beads. Alternatively, pour the warm juice into a flat pan and refrigerate for 1 hour. Cut into small cubes.

FOR THE CILANTRO-MINT PEARLS: Bring the water and salt to a boil in a small saucepan over medium-high heat. Add the cilantro, mint, and lime zest and blanch for 1 minute. Strain through a sieve and refrigerate until thoroughly chilled, about 1 hour. Once cold, transfer the herbs and zest to a blender and blend on high speed until the herbs become a green juice, adding water if necessary to thin. Strain through a sieve and chill again. In another small saucepan, thoroughly combine 1 cup of the herb juice with the agar-agar. Bring the mixture to a boil over medium-high heat, stirring constantly, then reduce the heat and simmer for 2 minutes until the agar-agar is dissolved completely. Dispense the warm herb juice drop by drop into the cold canola oil to form beads. Alternatively, pour the warm herb juice into a flat pan and refrigerate for 1 hour. Cut into small cubes.

FOR THE TOFU CEVICHE: In a medium bowl, mix the lemon juice, lime juice, salt, and tequila. Add the tofu cubes and refrigerate for 3 to 5 minutes. Drain and set aside.

FOR THE GARNISH: Cut the scallions into thin strips and put them in ice water to crisp. Drain, cover, and set aside. Pat the bell pepper dry with a paper towel and transfer to a bowl. Add the cucumber and mix well. Set aside.

To serve, spoon a little cucumber-pepper salad onto each plate. Place a few tofu ceviche cubes on top. Sprinkle with the pickled garlic and the mango and cilantro-mint pearls. Top the dish with a couple of strips of scallion and place a few tortilla chips on the side.

"This dish would make any vegan proud. It's packed with citrus and chili flavor, yet delicate in texture and appearance."

GAIL SIMMONS, **JUDGE**

MICHAEL V.'S HUEVOS CUBANOS

1 cup jasmine rice, rinsed

2½ cups water

Salt and freshly ground pepper

1 tablespoon extra-virgin olive oil

3 tablespoons unsalted butter

2 bananas, peeled and cut into thin slices

½ cup heavy cream

¼ cup vegetable oil

4 eggs

Red Tomato Jam (page 21) or 1 small tomato, cut into large dice, for serving

2 slices bacon, cooked until crisp then crumbled

10 fresh chives, minced

Prep time: 30 minutes

Season 6, Episode 11

Quickfire Challenge:
Create a breakfast in bed dish for Padma and guest judge Nigella Lawson. The winning recipe is featured in *Top Chef: The Quickfire Cookbook.* See www.chroniclebooks.com for more information.

SERVES 4

In a medium saucepan over medium-high heat, combine the rice, water, and a pinch of salt. Bring to a boil, reduce the heat to low, and simmer, covered, until the rice is tender, about 15 minutes. Remove from the heat and let the rice cool for at least 15 minutes. Using a ring mold or your hands, form the rice into four 3-inch circles or patties (you may have leftover rice).

Melt 2 tablespoons of the butter in a heavy skillet over medium heat. Cook without stirring until the milk solids have settled to the bottom of the pan and turned a light brown. Add the bananas and sauté until brown. Gently stir in the cream and cook until the bananas are tender, about 5 minutes. Carefully transfer the mixture to a blender and blend to a smooth purée.

Heat the oil in a large nonstick sauté pan over medium-high heat. Arrange the rice patties in the pan and fry until crispy, about 3 minutes per side. Drain on paper towels.

In a large nonstick skillet, melt the remaining 1 tablespoon butter over medium heat. Break the eggs into the pan and fry until the whites are just set, about 30 seconds. Continue to cook, shaking the pan gently, for 1 minute more. Then flip the eggs and cook for 1 minute longer.

To serve, spoon a circle of the banana purée onto each of 4 plates. Top the purée with a rice cake, top the rice cake with an egg, and mound the tomato jam to the side. Garnish with the bacon and chives.

LISA'S PAD THAI DEMO

Experienced New York chef Lisa Fernandes, who has been cooking in restaurant kitchens since she was a teenager, brought her Asian flavors and sharp technique to the table during Season 4. At times Lisa let stress get the better of her, and she became known for her serious temper. But that didn't stop her from making it all the way to the finals, where her sequence of exquisite Asian-inspired dishes did not fail to impress.

HOW TO PREPARE PAD THAI

Here are Lisa's instructions for one of her favorite Asian noodle dishes.

1. To make the sauce, cook down palm sugar with rice wine vinegar and fish sauce until almost a syrup.

2. Soak Thai rice noodles for about 30 minutes; don't let them get mushy.

3. Heat a large pan over high heat; heat canola oil until hot; add eggs and scramble.

4. Add shrimp, tofu, beef, and mixed vegetables to the pan and cook.

5. Drain the soaked noodles, add to the pan, and toss together until warmed through. Add the sauce and toss with the noodles until absorbed.

6. Add paprika and ground peanuts and toss. Remove from the heat, toss in minced cilantro and scallion, and serve.

Lisa's Magic Ingredient

- Fish sauce; it's key in a lot of dishes. It adds that special something. It smells horrible in the bottle, but it adds a smoky saltiness that goes a long way. To 2 cups of rice, you add ½ to 1 teaspoon. You don't want the food to taste like fish sauce.

"Asian cuisine is about balancing the sweet, sour, and salty; nothing too wet, nothing too dry."

CURRENT GIG: Working at Dos Caminos restaurant in Manhattan.

BIGGEST INFLUENCE: I get my palate from my mother, who can taste anything and guess what's in it. My mother learned from her mother—no one in my family went to culinary school.

BIGGEST KITCHEN NO-NO: What people fear most is undercooking or overcooking proteins.

THOUGHTS ON THE FINALE: I was proud of my meal in the finale. I showed my true colors, and I really brought out my personality in the food.

ANITA LO'S SOFT-SCRAMBLED EGG WITH SHIITAKES

WINNER!

4 eggs

1/3 cup heavy cream

1 tablespoon chopped fresh chives, plus chives chopped into 1-inch lengths for garnish (optional)

1 tablespoon oyster sauce, or as needed

Pinch of freshly ground pepper

3 tablespoons unsalted butter

4 shiitake mushroom caps, brushed clean and cut into small dice

SERVES 4

Snip off the tops of the eggs with an egg cutter. Discard the tops. Pour the eggs into a bowl. Rinse out the egg bottoms thoroughly with hot water and place upside down to dry.

Add the cream, chopped chives, oyster sauce, and pepper to the bowl with the eggs and whisk to blend.

In a medium sauté pan, melt the butter over high heat. Add the mushrooms and sauté until soft. Season with salt and pepper and transfer to a bowl. Pour the egg mixture into the pan and place over low heat. Slowly whisk the eggs to form small curds and cook until the whites are opaque but the eggs are still soft and creamy, 12 to 14 minutes.

To serve, spoon the scrambled eggs into the clean egg shell bottoms and garnish each serving with 2 or 3 chive pieces, if desired.

Prep time: 30 minutes

Top Chef Masters, Season 1, Episode 4

Quickfire Challenge: Create an egg dish using only one hand.

ANITA LO DISHES

"I was thinking that I might be able to crack those eggs with just one hand, but that was impossible and I ended up needing to get some help. I spent a lot of time trying to find something that the scrambled egg could sit on top of. I went through several different cups that didn't work, until I found the sake *masu*. When that happened, I decided I needed to make the dish Asian. Hence the shiitakes and the little touch of oyster sauce, which made it taste more Chinese."

"Anita had to slice the egg tops off in a very precise manner, and she literally needed a hand."

JOHN BESH, *TOP CHEF MASTERS* SEASON 1, CHEF

Q + A

stephanie

When Stephanie Izard arrived as a contestant for Season 4, she was already an experienced executive chef at her own restaurant, Scylla, in Chicago. She performed at a consistently high level throughout the competition, managing to keep her cool even while other chef'testants were losing it. Having worked with Jean-Georges Vongerichten and other big names, Stephanie developed a wide range of skills that—along with her focus and fortitude—helped her win the title of Top Chef.

What has life been like after the *Top Chef* win?
Crazy! I've been opening my restaurant, traveling all over, invading kitchens, meeting tons of great chefs and other fun people, doing various food and wine events and appearances, and just having a great time.

How did the show influence your cooking?
There has been more change to my cooking since being on the show. I met some talented chefs while filming and have met more along the way since, and my food just keeps evolving as with all chefs. You never stop learning.

Why is there so much drama on the show?
When you put fifteen or so strong personalities in a house together and take away normal sleep habits and, of course, add in alcohol, there is bound to be drama. I just tried to avoid it for the most part and did what I went there to do—cook.

What did you think of Season 5 and 6?
It has been fun to watch other seasons, though a bit bizarre. I will say I was not a fan of the romantic drama that made it on air for Season 5, as it takes away from the focus of the show. But otherwise it was fun to watch. I think Season 6 is a big step up as far as talent goes.

What did you think of *Top Chef Masters*? What was it like being at that finale meal?
I think it was great. It gave some well-known, established chefs who once judged us a chance to see how hard the competition really can be. Of course, they did not have to be sequestered for five weeks and live with one another, so they got off easy. Some of those chefs have so much going on that they do not get to be on the line anymore, so it was fun to see them actually cooking. As for the dinner, it was nice to be on the other side. I cannot believe the judges eat that much week in and week out.

What challenges would you have chef'testants do?
As a scuba diver, I would love to see them dive for their own fish and shellfish and cook on the beach. It's probably not going to happen though.

What can home cooks learn from the show?
It's tricky to follow the recipes as a home cook while watching the show, but now people can go to bravotv.com or buy one of the books and try some of the favorites. Just listening to the chefs and judges talk about the food and critique it can be very educational.

MIKE I.'S TUNA, PEARS, AND PONZU

TRUFFLE PONZU SAUCE

½ cup water

3 sheets *kombu*

1 small piece fresh ginger, peeled and sliced

½ cup bonito flakes

1 cup soy sauce

¼ cup rice vinegar

2 tablespoons mirin

2 tablespoons sugar

Juice of 1 lime

Juice of 1 lemon

Juice of 2 oranges

4 tablespoons summer truffles, minced

PICKLED ASIAN PEAR

½ cup vinegar

½ cup water

¼ cup sugar

1 serrano chile, seeded and cut into julienne

1 Asian pear, peeled, cored, and cut into julienne

....

TUNA

¼ cup extra-virgin olive oil

Juice of ½ orange

¼ cup rice vinegar

2 tablespoons honey

2 tablespoons soy sauce

2 teaspoons peeled and grated fresh ginger

2 teaspoons sesame oil

2 teaspoons sea salt

2 teaspoons *sambal oelek*

1 pound tuna loin, cut into 2-inch squares

2 teaspoons vegetable oil

Summer truffles for shaving for garnish

1 small bunch fresh chives, minced

SERVES 12

FOR THE PONZU SAUCE: In a small saucepan over medium heat, bring the water, *kombu*, and ginger to a simmer. Simmer for 20 minutes, then add the bonito flakes and continue to simmer for 5 minutes longer. Strain the liquid and refrigerate for 30 minutes. Combine the bonito stock with the soy sauce; vinegar; mirin; sugar; lime, lemon, and orange juices; and the truffles. Pass through a strainer and return to the refrigerator for at least 30 minutes or up to 2 hours.

FOR THE PICKLED ASIAN PEAR: In a small saucepan over medium heat, bring the vinegar, water, sugar, and chile to a simmer. Stir until the sugar dissolves. Place the pear in a small bowl, pour the vinegar mixture over it, and let cool completely.

FOR THE TUNA: In a small bowl, whisk together the olive oil, orange juice, vinegar, honey, soy sauce, ginger, sesame oil, sea salt, and *sambal* until smooth. Arrange the tuna in a large dish, cover with the marinade, and let stand at room temperature for at least 10 minutes and no longer than 20 minutes. Remove the tuna from the marinade and pat dry. Heat a large sauté pan over high heat. When it smokes, add the oil. Add the tuna and sear on all sides. Keep as rare as possible. Remove from the pan and chill immediately for at least 30 minutes.

To serve, place sauce, tuna, and pears in bowls. Garnish with truffles and chives.

🕐 Prep time: 2 hours, plus chilling

📺 Season 6, Episode 7

✎ Elimination Challenge:
Create a dish using only surprise ingredients.

DALE T. AND STEPHANIE'S SHRIMP, AÏOLI, AND PICKLED PEPPERS

DEVILED AÏOLI

2 eggs, hard boiled and peeled, whites discarded

1/2 teaspoon Dijon mustard

1 cup canola or grapeseed oil

1 tablespoon fresh lemon juice

1 1/2 teaspoons chile-garlic sauce such as Sriracha

1 teaspoon soy sauce

PICKLED PEPPERS

4 cups mixed hot and sweet peppers and chiles, such as red bell, jalapeño, banana, and gypsy, seeded

2 pounds English cucumbers, thinly shaved

1 1/2 cups rice vinegar

3/4 cup mirin

3/4 cup sugar

1 teaspoon salt

2 tablespoons sesame oil

FIRE-GRILLED SHRIMP

1/4 cup olive oil

4 cloves garlic, minced

1 tablespoon peeled and minced fresh ginger

2 teaspoons chile-garlic sauce such as Sriracha

1 pound jumbo shrimp, peeled and deveined

Salt and freshly ground pepper

Lisa's Miso Bacon (facing page) for serving

🕐 **Prep time:** 1 hour

🖵 Season 4, Episode 5

🔪 **Elimination Challenge:** Create a dish based on one of the classical elements: earth, fire, water, or air.

ABOUT A TECHNIQUE

pickling

When we think of pickling, we tend to think of onerous big barrels and sterilized jars. But a quick pickling of thinly sliced vegetables, such as chiles, cucumbers, or sweet red onions, is an easy way to add an acidic kick to any dish. Many world cuisines feature tangy pickles of various kinds, including kimchee in Korea, sweet and tangy pickles from India, and pickled cabbage slaw from El Salvador.

SERVES 3 OR 4

FOR THE DEVILED AÏOLI: Press the egg yolks through the small holes of a box grater. In a large bowl, whisk together the yolks and mustard. Add the oil in a slow drizzle, whisking constantly, until the mixture thickens to the consistency of mayonnaise. Stir in the lemon juice, chile-garlic sauce, and soy sauce. Refrigerate until serving.

FOR THE PICKLED PEPPERS: Using a mandoline, slice the peppers and chiles into 1/8-inch-wide rings. Rinse the rings repeatedly under running cold water to remove the seeds. Place the chile rings in a heatproof bowl, add the cucumbers, and toss to mix.

In a saucepan, combine the vinegar, mirin, sugar, and salt over high heat and bring to a simmer. Pour the hot vinegar mixture over the chile mixture. Let marinate at room temperature for 1 hour. Mix in the sesame oil.

FOR THE FIRE-GRILLED SHRIMP: In a small bowl, combine the olive oil, garlic, ginger, and chile-garlic sauce. Toss the shrimp with this mixture and marinate, refrigerated, for at least 1 hour.

Preheat a grill to high. Remove the shrimp from the marinade, season with salt and pepper, and grill until pink and cooked through, 2 to 3 minutes.

To serve, place a spoonful of the aïoli on each plate and top with the shrimp. Top with the pickled peppers, and lean a slice of miso bacon against the shrimp.

LISA'S MISO BACON

WINNER!

½ pound sliced bacon

½ cup *shiro* (white) miso

¼ cup pure maple syrup

1 cup rice vinegar

¾ cup mirin

SERVES 4 TO 8

Preheat the oven to 375°F.

Lay the bacon on a rimmed baking sheet lined with Silpat or parchment paper, with the slices slightly overlapping and all facing the same direction. Lay another Silpat or sheet of parchment on top and put a smaller baking sheet on top of that. Weight it down with a heavy, ovenproof pot. Bake until the bacon is crisp but not quite done, about 25 minutes. Remove the heavy pot and top pan. Remove the bacon from the oven but leave the oven on.

Meanwhile, in a large saucepan, combine the miso, maple syrup, vinegar, and mirin over medium-low heat. Whisk together and reduce until thick and glossy, about 25 minutes.

Lay the cooked bacon on a clean baking sheet lined with parchment paper. Glaze the bacon generously with the miso sauce. Return to the oven and bake until crisped, about 10 minutes longer. Let cool and cut lengthwise into even, long strips, about 1 by 4 inches.

🕐 **Prep time:** 35 minutes

📺 **Season 4, Episode 5**

🔪 **Elimination Challenge:** Create a dish based on one of the classical elements: earth, fire, water, or air.

ABOUT AN INGREDIENT

shiro miso

Miso, a staple of Japanese cooking, is a thick paste made from fermented soybeans, rice, barley, and/or other ingredients. It can be salty or sweet, and comes in many varieties. *Shiro* miso, or white miso, is the sweetest and mildest type. It combines beautifully with something as salty and rich as bacon.

"The glaze gives you this gooey, sticky miso flavor that completely changes the character of the bacon."

LISA, SEASON 4

RADHIKA'S JERK HALIBUT WITH MANGO SLAW

JERK HALIBUT

1 tablespoon Jerk Seasoning
(below)

1 teaspoon olive oil

4 halibut fillets, about 6 ounces each

Salt and freshly ground pepper

....

MINT-CILANTRO VINAIGRETTE

1/2 cup coarsely chopped
fresh cilantro

1/2 cup coarsely chopped fresh mint

1/2-inch piece fresh ginger,
peeled and chopped

3/4 cup extra-virgin olive oil

3/4 cup rice vinegar

1/2 teaspoon sugar

1/2 tablespoon fresh lime juice

Salt and freshly ground pepper

....

MANGO SLAW

1 mango, peeled, pitted, and
cut into julienne

1/4 cup chopped fresh cilantro

Salt and freshly ground pepper

RICE

2 teaspoons olive oil

1 small onion, diced

1 clove garlic, minced

1 tablespoon tomato paste

1 tablespoon Jamaican curry paste

1 cup long-grain rice

2 cups water

....

Plantain or taro chips for garnish

SERVES 4

FOR THE JERK HALIBUT: In a small bowl, whisk together the jerk spice and 1 teaspoon of the olive oil. Rub the marinade all over the halibut, cover, and refrigerate for at least 30 minutes.

FOR THE MINT-CILANTRO VINAIGRETTE: In a blender, purée the cilantro, mint, ginger, olive oil, vinegar, sugar, and lime juice, until smooth. Season with salt and pepper.

FOR THE MANGO SLAW: In a bowl, toss together the mango, cilantro, and three-fourths of the vinaigrette. Season with salt and pepper and set aside.

FOR THE RICE: In a medium saucepan, heat the olive oil over medium-high heat. Add the onion and garlic and sauté until translucent. Mix in the tomato paste and Jamaican curry powder, then add the rice and sauté until toasted. Add the water, bring to a boil, cover, turn the heat down to low, and cook until the rice is tender, about 15 minutes.

Meanwhile, heat the remaining 1 teaspoon olive oil in a heavy skillet over medium-high heat. Add the fish and panfry until lightly browned, about 5 minutes per side.

To serve, place a small mound of rice in the center of each of 4 plates, and arrange a fillet on top of each mound. Top with the mango slaw. Drizzle with the vinaigrette and top with the plantain chips.

Prep time: 2 hours

Season 5, Episode 1

Elimination Challenge:
Create a dish that represents the ethnic cuisine of a New York neighborhood.

HOW TO MAKE

jerk seasoning

1 teaspoon salt
1 teaspoon ground allspice
1 teaspoon sugar
1 teaspoon dried thyme
1 teaspoon freshly ground black pepper
1/2 teaspoon cayenne pepper
1/4 teaspoon ground cinnamon
1/4 teaspoon freshly grated nutmeg

Combine all the ingredients. Store in an airtight container for up to 2 months.

WINNER!

KEVIN'S CHICKEN MOLE NEGRO

CHICKEN

2 boneless, skin-on chicken breasts, about 6 ounces each

2 ancho chiles, seeded

2 *pasilla negra* chiles, seeded

2 *guajillo chiles*, seeded

2 *morita* chiles, seeded

2 boneless, skinless chicken thighs, about 1 pound

4 slices bacon

Salt and freshly ground pepper

FIG JAM

5 fresh figs, stemmed and halved

1/2 cup hot strong-brewed coffee

1/4 cup hot chocolate

SEED PURÉE

3 tablespoons olive oil

1/4 cup sunflower seeds

2 tablespoons pumpkin seeds

1 red bell pepper, roasted, peeled, and seeded

1 plum (Roma) tomato, halved and charred

1 clove garlic, peeled

2 tablespoons water

1 teaspoon sherry vinegar

🕐 **Prep time:** 2 hours; make 1 day ahead

🖵 Season 6, Episode 6

🔪 Elimination Challenge: Deconstruct a vintage recipe and reimagine its components into a signature dish.

TOP CHEF

SERVES 4

FOR THE CHICKEN: Wrap the chicken breasts in plastic wrap and place in the refrigerator.

Place the chiles in a small bowl and cover with hot water. Soak until soft, about 30 minutes. Drain the chiles and set aside.

Place the chicken thighs and bacon in a food processor or meat grinder. Grind until the texture is fine and smooth. Transfer to a bowl. Drain the chiles and place in a food processor. Process to a smooth purée. Add the chile purée to the ground chicken and season with 1/2 teaspoon salt and 1/2 teaspoon pepper. Wrap the meat in plastic wrap and roll into a sausage-shaped log about 12 inches long and 2 inches in diameter. Tightly twist the ends to secure, and refrigerate the sausage for at least 8 hours or up to overnight.

Preheat the oven to 325°F.

Place the chicken sausage, still in its plastic wrapper, in a roasting pan filled with hot water. Poach in the oven until the chicken is opaque and the roll is firm to the touch, about 40 minutes. Remove from the oven, take the sausage out of the water, and let rest until cool enough to handle. Unwrap the sausage and slice into bite-sized pieces.

Raise the oven temperature to 425°F.

Season the chicken breasts with salt and pepper, rubbing the seasoning under and over the skin. Place in a baking pan and roast until opaque throughout and the juices run clear when the breast is pricked with a fork at the thickest part, 15 to 20 minutes.

FOR THE FIG JAM: In a medium bowl, combine the figs, coffee, and chocolate. Let the figs steep at room temperature for about 30 minutes. Drain the figs, reserving the liquid. Transfer the figs to a food processor and purée until smooth, adding some of the reserved liquid if necessary. Season with salt to taste and keep warm.

FOR THE SEED PURÉE: Heat 1 tablespoon of the olive oil in a small sauté pan over medium heat and toast the sunflower and pumpkin seeds until golden and fragrant, 3 to 5 minutes. Transfer the seeds to a food processor and add the roasted red pepper, tomato, and garlic. Process to a smooth purée, adding water 1 tablespoon at a time as needed to keep the mixture loose. Transfer to a bowl and mix in the sherry vinegar and the remaining 2 tablespoons olive oil. Keep warm.

To serve, smear a line of seed purée on a plate and top with a spoonful of fig jam. Position a sausage slice next to the jam and place 2 slices of chicken breast next to the sausage. Combine all elements in each bite.

ABOUT A TECHNIQUE

deconstructed cuisine

To deconstruct a dish means taking the concept, turning it upside down and inside out, and really reconceptualizing it. Chicken *mole* is traditionally served as roasted chicken parts with a deep, rich sauce that includes toasted chiles, chocolate, and pumpkin seeds. Kevin retained the core ingredients but reworked them so that what appears on the plate looks completely original, but still evokes the taste memory of a true mole.

"I'm good at thinking on my feet. We change the menu in my restaurant every day, so I'm accustomed to coming up with new stuff rapidly."

KEVIN, SEASON 6

DALE T.'S TEMPURA DEMO

Though he fell short of the finals in Season 4, Dale Talde impressed the judges with his consistently strong work in the kitchen, especially when it came to Asian-inspired dishes, such as his Tandoori Pork Ribs (facing page), which was voted winner of the Chicago Bears Tailgate Challenge.

"The best food doesn't need to be described or explained. The explanation should be on the plate."

HOT COOKING: Right now I am really into cooking directly over hot, hot heat, caveman style.

FAVORITE DISH FROM THE SEASON: My halo-halo was money. It had salty, sweet . . . a spectrum of flavors that is more difficult to do in dessert than in savory dishes.

ON *TOP CHEF MASTERS*: You thought it was so easy? You can't even get a plate out. I love it. When was the last time any of these chefs were deep in the juice, with no army of sous-chefs to help them out?

GO-TO INGREDIENTS:
- Oyster sauce and fish sauce
- *Calamansi*, a citrus fruit from the Philippines.

HOW TO PREPARE TEMPURA

Tempura was used to great effect during the Improv Challenge when Dale and Richard B. collaborated on the winning dish, Fried Tofu and Eggplant with Green Curry. Use caution when trying this at home; the cornstarch slurry coating will spatter when it hits the very hot oil.

1. Bring 1 gallon water to a boil and slowly stir in 1 cup cornstarch until thickened. Let the mixture cool until it forms a gel.

2. Take whatever ingredients you want to fry (my favorites are soft-shell crab and small fish), season them with salt and pepper, and rub the gel around them like a casing.

3. Apply dry cornstarch to the outside of the gel to seal it. Add the tempura coating just before frying so it won't get soggy.

4. Pour about 3 inches of canola oil into a deep, heavy-bottomed saucepan and heat to 400°F.

5. Carefully add the prepared food to the oil, working in batches to avoid crowding.

6. Fry, prodding with a skimmer, for up to a few minutes, depending on what you're cooking.

7. When it's done, the outside will be white and lacy, not golden.

Dale's Tools for Deep-Frying

- Deep fryer, deep-frying thermometer, skimmer, and paper towels

DALE T.'S TANDOORI PORK RIBS

WINNER!

1 tablespoon garam masala

1 tablespoon ground coriander

1 tablespoon Madras curry powder

2 cardamom pods

1½ teaspoons mustard seeds

1½ teaspoons ground white pepper

1 tablespoon chili powder

2 cups plus 1 tablespoon hot-pepper sauce

3 cups plain yogurt

¼ cup soy sauce

1 teaspoon salt

3 racks pork spareribs, about 3 pounds each

½ cup vinegar

¼ cup sugar

Peel of 1 fresh pineapple (reserve the fruit for another use)

SERVES 6 TO 8

Toast the garam masala, coriander, curry, cardamom, mustard seeds, white pepper, and chili powder in a medium skillet over medium heat until fragrant, about 1 minute. Transfer the spices to a blender and add 2 cups of the hot-pepper sauce, the yogurt, soy sauce, and salt. Blend until well combined. Set aside.

Trim any excess fat and remove the silver skin from the ribs. In a large pot or Dutch oven over medium-high heat, combine the ribs, vinegar, sugar, the remaining 1 tablespoon hot-pepper sauce, and the pineapple peel. Add cold water to cover. Bring to a boil, then reduce the heat to low and simmer, covered, until the meat is tender, about 2 hours. Remove the ribs from the liquid and set aside to cool.

Once the meat has cooled, place in a shallow dish or pan with half of the spicy yogurt and turn to coat thoroughly.

Preheat a grill to medium and lightly oil the grill rack. Remove the ribs from the marinade and cook on the grill until nicely brown, about 5 minutes per side.

To serve, pass the ribs with the remaining spicy yogurt on the side.

Prep time: 4 hours

Season 4, Episode 6

Elimination Challenge:
Cook a dish for a tailgate party.

DALE T. DISHES

"When I went into the challenge I thought, I'm going to make angry chicken wings. But Spike took all the wings. Instead I got pork ribs, and I had no more money to spend on anything else. So I used the ends of Spike's pineapple and threw it in the pot to ensure the ribs would be tender. If Spike knew what I was doing, he probably would never have given me the pineapple ends."

"The flavors were very unusual for tailgate food, but they really came together."

GAIL SIMMONS, **JUDGE**

MICHAEL V.'S BRAISED PORK BELLY WITH ROMAINE

1 slab smoked bacon (about 2½ pounds)

½ cup sesame oil

2 onions, sliced

2 carrots, peeled and diced

3 ribs celery, chopped

4 tablespoons ground ginger

2 cups soy sauce

½ cup whole-grain mustard

¼ cup prepared yellow mustard

½ cup honey

2 cups water

½ cup mango chutney

½ cup cornstarch

1 large head romaine lettuce, cored, separated into individual leaves, and spun dry

Spicy Peanuts (below)

SERVES 6 TO 8

Preheat the oven to 275°F.

Score the slab of bacon, creating cross-cut squares on the surface of the skin but being careful not to cut through to the meat. In a large Dutch oven, heat the sesame oil over medium-high heat and sear the bacon, scored side down, until well browned, about 10 minutes. Turn the bacon and add the onions, carrots, and celery and sauté for 2 minutes. Pour in water to come halfway up the sides of the meat. Add 2 table-spoons of the ground ginger. Cover the pot and braise in the oven until fork-tender, about 2½ hours.

Meanwhile, mix together the soy sauce, both mustards, honey, the remaining 2 tablespoons ground ginger, and 1 cup of the water in a medium saucepan. Bring to a simmer and cook to reduce the liquid by half, about 20 minutes. Stir in the mango chutney, remove from the heat, and set aside.

In a bowl, stir together the cornstarch with the remaining 1 cup water until it is dissolved.

Return the saucepan with soy-mustard mixture to medium heat. Add the cornstarch slurry in small increments, whisking constantly, until the mixture thickens enough to coat a spoon (you may not need all of the slurry).

Remove the pork belly from the oven and carefully lift it from the braising pot. Place it on a large platter, brush with the soy-mustard glaze, and slice thinly.

To serve, divide the lettuce leaves among individual plates. Top each leaf with a slice or two of the pork belly. Spoon more glaze over the pork and then sprinkle with the Spicy Peanuts.

🕐 **Prep time:** 30 minutes, plus braising

📺 Season 6, Episode 3

🔪 **Elimination Challenge:**
Create a dish to serve 300 airmen using only the supplies and equipment from a mess hall.

HOW TO MAKE

spicy peanuts

1 cup roasted peanuts, crushed

1 teaspoon ground ginger

¼ teaspoon cayenne pepper

Toss the peanuts with the ginger and cayenne.

EUGENE'S LAMB MASALA

TZATZIKI RICE

2 cups basmati rice, rinsed

3 cups cold water

1/2 red onion, diced

4 fresh chives, chopped

4 scallions, thinly sliced

1 cup raw, unsalted macadamia nuts, chopped

1/2 cup golden raisins

Juice of 1 lemon

2 cups plain yogurt

Salt and freshly ground pepper

LAMB

2 racks of lamb (about 16 chops)

1 cup garam masala

1/2 teaspoon salt

1 teaspoon freshly ground pepper

CURRY-MISO EMULSION

1/2 teaspoon canola oil

1/2 teaspoon peeled and minced fresh ginger

1/2 teaspoon minced garlic

Leaves from 1 small bunch fresh cilantro, chopped

1 1/2 cups vegetable stock or low-sodium broth

1/2 teaspoon curry powder

1/2 teaspoon garam masala (below)

1/2 teaspoon cayenne pepper

1/2 cup heavy cream

1/2 cup *aka* (red) miso

1/2 teaspoon garlic powder

SERVES 8 TO 10

FOR THE TZATZIKI RICE: Place the rice in a small saucepan. Add the water and bring to a boil over medium-high heat. Reduce the heat, cover, and simmer, until almost tender, 12 minutes. Remove from the heat and set aside, still covered, for 10 to 15 minutes.

In a large bowl, combine the onion, chives, scallions, nuts, raisins, and lemon juice, and toss to mix. Add the rice and yogurt and mix well. Season with salt and pepper.

FOR THE LAMB: Rub the lamb with the garam masala, salt, and pepper. Preheat a grill to medium-high.

Grill the lamb racks until medium-rare, about 15 minutes. Let rest for 5 to 10 minutes before slicing.

FOR THE CURRY-MISO EMULSION: In a small saucepan, heat the oil over medium-high heat and sauté the ginger, garlic, and cilantro until soft. Add the vegetable stock and bring to a boil. Reduce the heat and cook until the liquid is reduced by one-fourth. Add the curry powder, garam masala, cayenne, and cream and simmer until reduced by half. Transfer to a blender, add the miso and garlic powder, and blend until the sauce is emulsified. Strain into a clean saucepan and set aside.

To serve, place a large dollop of the rice in the center of each plate and arrange 3 chops on each mound. Ladle a little of the curry-miso emulsion around the lamb.

Prep time: 1 hour

Season 5, Episode 1

Elimination Challenge:
Create a dish that represents the ethnic cuisine of a New York neighborhood.

HOW TO MAKE

garam masala

4 tablespoons coriander seeds
1 tablespoon cumin seeds
1 tablespoon black peppercorns
2 teaspoons ground ginger
1 teaspoon ground cinnamon
1 teaspoon crushed bay leaves
3 or 4 black cardamom pods

Combine all the spices except the cardamom in a skillet and roast over medium-low heat, stirring occasionally, until fragrant. Open the cardamom pods to release the seeds into the mixture and grind to a fine powder in a spice grinder or clean coffee grinder. Store in an airtight container for up to 2 months.

ADVANCED
CULINARY APPLICATIONS:
TOP CHEF EXTREME

159

167

175

171

155

TOP PLATING

Top Chef has taught us that the way the food is arranged and presented on the plate has as much impact as the flavor of the dish. When it comes to presentation, begin by thinking about color and composition. Are there contrasting colors on the plate? Does it look overcrowded or fresh and appetizing? To take it a step further, invest in some inexpensive items like stainless-steel rings and a plastic squeeze bottle, and next thing you know you'll be turning out *Top Chef*–caliber dishes.

Plating Rings and Molds

These stainless-steel rings come in all sizes. They allow you to make neat, round stacks of various foods, which can chill in the mold and then remain upright without mushing together. They work best with any kind of food that is soft and pliable, such as guacamole, risotto, mashed vegetables, and mousses.

Fun with Garnishes

Garnishes should be edible and should tie into whatever the dish is. It's always nice to have some crunch or texture in a garnish. When in doubt, a sprinkle of finely minced fresh parsley works well on top of nearly everything. For desserts, try shaving chocolate directly over the plate with a peeler, or spoon over diced strawberry macerated in sugar or liqueur.

The Smear

To make a decorative smear, make sure you have a large white plate as a backdrop (this will enhance the visual kick). Take a thick sauce or purée and gently smear it from one side of the plate to the other, using a small icing knife.

Squeeze Bottle

Instead of spooning (or pouring) sauce onto a plate, put it in a simple plastic squeeze bottle and you can exert total control over where it goes and what it looks like. Use the bottle to create dots, hatch marks, squiggly lines—whatever inspires you. The squeeze bottle works well with slightly thick sauces.

Dusting

Chefs have long dusted desserts with a shower of confectioners' sugar or cocoa. You will also find plates dusted with spices such as paprika or cayenne. Place the powder in a fine sieve and shake over your plate. For a more delicate hand, place the spices in a spice grinder and grind onto the plate.

Duos and Trios

Several chefs have been shot down by the judges for creating showy duos or trios for no reason other than that they look cool. The ring mold works wonders for making a duo or trio (or more), though it's not a necessity. Start with a large, white rectangular dish, and place small bits down at intervals on the plate.

MICHAEL V.'S NITRO GAZPACHO

WINNER!

4 ripe tomatoes, chopped

1 red bell pepper, seeded and chopped

1 clove garlic, chopped

¼ cup sherry vinegar

½ cucumber, peeled and chopped

10 leaves of fresh basil

2 tablespoons sugar

½ cup extra-virgin olive oil

Salt

Liquid nitrogen

GARNISH

4 sprigs fresh basil

Olive oil for drizzling

¼ cucumber, peeled and cut into sticks

2 slices white bread, toasted and cut diagonally

Prep time: 15 minutes

Season 6, Episode 2

Quickfire Challenge:
Create a dish with the same number of ingredients as you rolled at the craps table.

SERVES 4

Combine the tomatoes, bell pepper, garlic, vinegar, cucumber, basil, and sugar in a bowl. Transfer the ingredients to a blender and, with the motor running, stream in the olive oil to emulsify the soup. Season with salt. Transfer the soup to a stand mixer and, on low speed, add liquid nitrogen until frozen.

To serve, garnish the gazpacho with a sprig of basil, a drizzle of olive oil, a cucumber stick, and a triangle of toast.

"My brother Bryan is a little more conservative than I am. I'm more likely to take some risks."

MICHAEL V., SEASON 6 WINNER

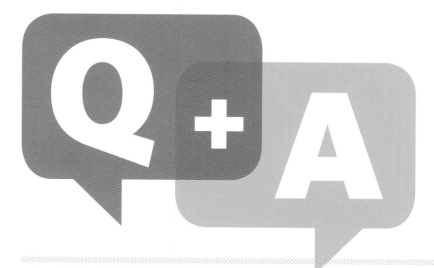

WITH
wylie dufresne

The culinary genius behind New York's wd~50, Wylie Dufresne is known for creative cooking of the highest level. He appeared as a guest judge during Seasons 4 and 5, where he was greeted like a rock star by the admiring chef'testants, before joining the competition himself in *Top Chef Masters*. He used a Dr Pepper reduction to accompany his grilled cheese sandwich in the Quickfire Challenge. In the elimination round, he narrowly lost to Suzanne Tracht with his creative roasted chicken dish and magical slow-poached egg.

What have you been up to lately?

It's been a good year. At wd~50, we're always working on new ideas and new concepts. We're particularly proud of the aerated foie on the menu right now. It's a foie gras terrine that, while still fluid, is sealed in a container with a one-way valve and then exposed to a partial vacuum, then allowed to set. This creates a network of air bubbles throughout the terrine, lightening the texture.

What was it like being on the other side as a competitor on *Top Chef Masters*?

It gives you perspective, like anything when the shoe is on the other foot. It gives you a real understanding of time constraints and what one has to work with.

What made you want to become a chef?

If I had had the aptitude for it, I would have liked to be an athlete. But I was not particularly gifted in that respect, and I found that working in a kitchen gave me a similar satisfaction. Also, my father has been involved in the industry for most of his life, so I grew up in that environment.

How did you first become interested in molecular gastronomy?

First and foremost we need to insert a disclaimer regarding molecular gastronomy. I think it's a misleading term, but I can't offer you a more satisfactory one either. I feel that it does more of a disservice to scientists than to chefs. The term was coined by scientists to define their work with regard to explaining the scientific principles involved in the cooking process. What led me to the approach we use at wd~50 was trying to understand what we do in a deeper way. It's like any discipline; you want to explore it in as much depth as you can. What you call molecular gastronomy, I see more as learning and understanding.

What advice do you have for home cooks who are interested in avant-garde techniques?

If people want to cook at home in creative ways that's great. It's not just powders. Liquid nitrogen, used properly, is no more dangerous than an open flame; it's just unfamiliar. There's a huge library to be consulted.

HUBERT KELLER'S CARROT-CARDAMOM FONDANT

WINNER!

2 cups fresh carrot juice

3 tablespoons powdered gelatin

1 teaspoon rice wine vinegar

1 teaspoon cracked cardamom

Salt and freshly ground pepper

Pinch of sugar (optional)

¼ cup heavy whipping cream, beat into stiff peaks

2 ounces caviar, preferably black, such as osetra

8 sprigs fresh chervil

MAKES 8 SHOOTERS, 2 OUNCES EACH

Pour the carrot juice into a medium nonreactive saucepan and stir in the gelatin. Add the vinegar, cardamom, salt and pepper to taste, and a pinch of sugar, if desired. Bring the mixture to a boil, stirring continuously, then reduce the heat and simmer gently for 10 minutes. Turn off the heat, cover the pan, and let the cardamom infuse the liquid for 10 minutes longer. Taste and adjust the seasoning, adding more sugar to balance out the acid of the vinegar if necessary. Strain the carrot juice and allow to cool until the liquid is a thick gelée. Divide the carrot gelée among 8 shooter glasses and place in the refrigerator until fully set, about 2 hours.

To serve, season the whipped cream with a pinch of salt and pepper. Drop a dollop of the cream on top of each shooter glass. Top the cream with the caviar and garnish with a sprig of chervil.

🕐 **Prep time:** 30 minutes, plus chilling

📺 *Top Chef Masters*, Season 1, Episode 9

🔪 **Elimination Challenge:** Create a buffet for 200 guests with a team of three sous-chefs.

SHOOTERS

Gelatin shooters started out as a way to get very drunk very fast, allowing sweetened vodka to slip down one's throat with the greatest of ease. Now shooters have gone highbrow. Chefs have discovered that a petite shot glass is the perfect vessel for an *amuse-bouche* or appetizer. Here, a spice-infused carrot juice is set with gelatin and then topped with osetra caviar.

"Everybody loves Chef Keller. Everybody wants to work with him."

BETTY, SEASON 2

Q+A

WITH
john besh

Chef John Besh, a James Beard award winner and the owner of August, Besh Steak, La Provence, and Domenica, all in New Orleans, lent his expertise to the judging table for the Season 5 finale. He returned to don his whites for a good cause in *Top Chef Masters*, but was so busy being affable and easygoing in the kitchen that he nearly didn't get his slow-cooked eggs out in time.

What was it like being a guest judge on the Season 5 finale?

I had such a great time working on that show at Commanders Palace. Hosea, Stefan, and Carla were completely different, and each one stood out so well. I was impressed. You could see that Stefan was technically gifted, and at first I expected him to be the one to beat. But Stefan was playing it safe that day, and Hosea was hitting for the bleachers—and he nailed it.

Hosea really worked New Orleans flavors and soul into his food, and he made the main ingredient in each dish really shine. I thought I was going to hate his blackened red fish, and it was one of the best bites of my life. He deserved the win. Poor Carla made one blunder. A couple of the things she did outshone everybody. But her blue cheese soufflé did not work at all. Oh heck, that really put her behind.

What was it like to be a participant?

With *Top Chef Masters*, I knew what I was getting into, and I felt like I didn't have anything to prove. I did it for the charitable aspect. I had done a lot of other challenge shows, but I underestimated the time I needed, and I was paying attention to other things. But to have the opportunity to hang with those professionals was a lot of fun.

How would you describe your style of cooking?

My style of cooking is contemporary Louisiana French. Being that we have such a distinct culture, I always want to pay homage to it. I want to honor New Orleans cuisine and play within it. All my cooking is within that context, which gives me an awful lot of leeway because we have French, Caribbean, Spanish, and Italian. All these people came and left an ingredient in this gumbo pot. Creole is the only indigenous urban cuisine in the country. As a New Orleans chef, I need to be a steward of traditional cuisine and also push it forward.

What are your top five ingredients for New Orleans cooking?

Blue crabs, shrimp, andouille sausage, crawfish, okra.

Can you share a technique you use?

I'll make a shrimp stock or a crab stock, and I'll reduce it down with some cream or vermouth and freeze it in small amounts at home. Then, on a weeknight, I can take out a portion and add a little mustard and a little butter and tarragon, and I have a beautiful sauce.

JOHN BESH'S FROZEN CAULIFLOWER BLINTZ

1 head cauliflower, trimmed, cored, and coarsely chopped

1 potato, peeled and quartered

1/2 cup heavy cream, plus more as needed

1/2 cup chicken stock or low-sodium broth

2 tablespoons unsalted butter

Salt and freshly ground pepper

Black truffle for shaving

8 ounces smoked salmon, cut into julienne

SERVES 4

In a medium saucepan, combine the cauliflower and potato and add water to cover. Bring to a boil and cook over medium-high heat until tender, 12 to 15 minutes. Drain thoroughly, transfer the cauliflower and potatoes to a blender, add the cream, chicken stock, and butter, and purée just until the mixture is thick enough to coat the back of a spoon. Thin with more cream, if needed. Season with salt, pepper, and black truffle shavings.

Spoon small mounds of the cauliflower mixture onto an antigriddle and let set, about 20 seconds. Flip the mound over with a nonmetal spatula and let set on the other side, then remove the mounds from the griddle.

ALTERNATIVE METHOD—Thoroughly chill the cauliflower mixture in the refrigerator or freezer, then transfer it to an ice-cream maker and freeze according to the manufacturer's instructions. Transfer the ice cream to round ice-cube trays and freeze to set the shape.

To serve, place the frozen cauliflower blintzes on plates and top with the salmon.

 Prep time: 45 minutes, plus chilling

Top Chef Masters, Season 1, Episode 4

Elimination Challenge: Create a dish inspired by a magic word: mystery, surprise, spectacle, or illusion.

ABOUT A TECHNIQUE

antigriddle

Inspired by innovative chef and *Top Chef* guest judge Grant Achatz, the antigriddle is a nifty machine about the size of a bread box, with a cold metal plate on top that instantly flash freezes or semifreezes foods. The gizmo allows chefs to play with contrasting textures and temperatures in ways that would not have been possible before.

> "I'm creating a dish designed to surprise the diners with textures and flavors that they wouldn't expect would work together."

JOHN BESH, *TOP CHEF MASTERS* SEASON 1, CHEF

KEVIN'S PORK TERRINE WITH PICKLED CHERRIES

WINNER!

MUSHROOM MAYONNAISE

2 tablespoons unsalted butter

1 pound shiitake mushrooms, brushed clean and stemmed

1 pound button mushrooms, brushed clean

6 ounces dried morel mushrooms, soaked in hot water for 30 minutes

8 ounces oyster mushrooms, brushed clean

3/4 cup hazelnut flour

2 tablespoons minced shallots

2 egg yolks

1 1/2 tablespoons fresh lemon juice

3/4 cup rendered pork fat

Leaves from 1 bunch fresh flat-leaf parsley, chopped

Salt and freshly ground pepper

PORK TERRINE

1/2 pound fatback, sliced

1 egg

2 tablespoons all-purpose flour

1/4 cup heavy cream

1 tablespoon brandy

2 1/2 pounds ground pork

1 cup chopped fresh flat-leaf parsley

1 tablespoon *quatre épices*

2 tablespoons salt

Pickled Cherries (below) for serving

SERVES 8 TO 10

FOR THE MUSHROOM MAYONNAISE: In a large sauté pant, melt the butter over medium-high heat and cook the mushrooms until deep brown. Set aside.

Heat a small sauté pan over medium heat and toast the hazelnut flour with the shallots. Remove the pan from the burner and set aside.

In a medium bowl, combine the egg yolks and lemon juice and whisk together until thick and almost white. Slowly drizzle in the rendered pork fat while whisking constantly until the mayonnaise is thick. Fold the mayonnaise into the mushrooms and transfer to a food processor. Pulse the mixture just until combined and transfer to a bowl. Fold in the parsley and season with salt and pepper. Cover and refrigerate.

FOR PORK TERRINE: Preheat the oven to 300°F.

Line the bottom and long sides of a 9-by-3-inch terrine mold with the fatback slices. Arrange the slices close together and be sure to leave an overhang.

Mix together the egg, flour, cream, and brandy in a large bowl. Fold in the pork, parsley, *quatre epices*, and salt until well combined. Pack the meat mixture into the terrine mold, making sure all crevices are filled (rap the mold to ensure it is compact). Fold over the fatback to cover the meat mixture. Bake for 1 1/4 hours. Remove from oven, let cool, cover, and refrigerate overnight before serving.

To serve, spread the pickled cherries on each plate, place a slice of the terrine on top, and drop a dollop of mushroom mayonnaise on the terrine.

Prep time: 2 hours, plus 1 day for setting

Season 6, Episode 8

Elimination Challenge: Create a dish using a designated cut of pork, and pair it with a Pinot Noir.

HOW TO MAKE

pickled cherries

1 cup sugar

2 cups red wine vinegar

1 cinnamon stick

1 star anise pod

Salt

2 cups fresh or frozen Bing cherries, pitted and quartered

In a small saucepan, combine the sugar, vinegar, cinnamon stick, star anise, and salt to taste and bring to a boil over medium-high heat. Add the cherries and remove the pan from the heat. Let the fruit cool to room temperature, then refrigerate until needed.

RICHARD B.'S DRY-ICE CREAM DEMO

From the very first episode of Season 4, Richard Blais announced himself as an experienced chef who's not afraid to throw in a little "shock and awe." From his hand-smoker, used in his Crab Cakes (page 162), to his Salmon with "Caviar" (page 171), to the liquid nitrogen used to make his signature Banana Scallops, Richard knows how to give cooking an avant-garde kick.

HOW TO MAKE DRY-ICE CREAM

Richard's Atlanta hamburger joint, Flip, may be the only diner in America where the shakes are created with liquid nitrogen. Don't try this at home unless you feel comfortable working with dry ice.

1 cup milk left over from your favorite cereal

1 cup half-and-half

Glucose (optional)

Xanthan gum (optional)

2 tablespoons sugar

Dry ice, pulverized to a fine powder

1. In a small saucepan over low heat, combine the milk, half-and-half, sugar, and glucose. Heat until the sugar is dissolved.

2. Off the burner, with an immersion blender, buzz in the xanthan gum and then strain through a fine-mesh sieve. Chill the mixture until cool.

3. Put the ice-cream base in a stand mixer fitted with the whisk attachment. On low speed, slowly add the dry ice powder (it will make a dramatic smoke), then continue to beat until the mixture is the consistency of ice cream.

Special Instructions

- Always handle dry ice with caution, as it can burn your hands and tongue. Gloves and safety goggles are recommended.

- To pulverize the dry ice, smash it with a hammer inside a plastic bag, then pulse it in a food processor.

- The ice cream will be very cold. Let it sit at room temperature before serving to avoid burning your tongue.

TOOLS OF THE TOP CHEF KITCHEN BY RICHARD B.

As the show becomes more popular and as more chefs with diverse cooking styles come on each season, the kitchen gets upgraded. If a chef'testant introduces an ingredient or tool, it seems destined to appear in the next season's pantry. Here are some of the tools that have been added.

1. Vacuum Packer

Popularized by Hung in Season 3, the vacuum is crucial to sous-vide cooking. This technology allows you to infuse, marinate, compress, cook sous-vide, and store ingredients efficiently. The Season 6 kitchen was equipped with a high-powered industrial model for the first time. Bryan used the technology of the vacuum chamber to cook his black cod sous-vide.

The Tech Shelf

This shelf includes ingredients used in the modern kitchen that previously could only be brought in secretly by chef'testants. They range from methyl cellulose (used to make Bryan's macarons, page 25) to glucono delta-lactone. Look for these jars and containers filled with nondescript whitish powders to emulsify, gel, dry, encapsulate, acidulate, carbonate, and basically manipulate many preparations.

2. Poly-Science Immersion Circulator

A favorite of multiple chef'testants and used extensively in serious professional kitchens, the immersion circulator will hold a precise temperature, allowing you to cook with precision to a tenth of a degree. The circulator warms a "bath" where vacuum-sealed ingredients float and slowly cook. It is the most common tool used in cooking sous-vide. I liken it to a high-tech Crock-Pot, or maybe a Jacuzzi.

iSi Siphons or "Foam Canisters"

Popularized by Marcel in Season 2, these containers can carbonate, inflate, aerate, chill, and basically manipulate to create airy textures and melting mouthfeels. Once available only as a chef's secret piece of equipment, they are now readily at our chefs' disposal in the storage area.

3. Liquid Nitrogen

What was made available to me only in a soup thermos in Puerto Rico is now available in the form of a 600-pound pressurized tank and a transportable container for the chef'testants to take on the road. Liquid nitrogen allows you to freeze anything in minutes or even seconds. It creates amazing texture and therefore mouthfeel (see Michael V.'s Nitro Gazpacho, page 152). It can also be used to freeze alcohol, as in Michael V.'s Apple Sorbet (page 189).

Along with these tools, also look for pressure cookers (in my opinion, the most important piece of equipment in the kitchen), multiple small smoking units (as used by Hector in the first Quickfire Challenge of Season 6), anti-griddles (used by John Besh for his Frozen Cauliflower Blintz, page 157), dehydrators, and Pacojet frozen-food processors!

RICHARD B.'S SMOKED CRAB CAKES

CRAB CAKES

1 crab (about 8 ounces), steamed

Canola oil

1/4 teaspoon celery salt

1/4 teaspoon fennel seeds

Salt and freshly ground pepper

1/3 cup water

2 cups apple cider

1 pound fresh lump crabmeat

1/2 cup mayonnaise

1 small onion, minced

4 fresh chives, minced

Pinch of smoke powder

Ras el hanout (page 118)

Unsalted butter

BRUSSELS SPROUT SALAD

10 Brussels sprouts

3 tablespoons mustard-seed pickle

1 green apple, cored and diced

🕐 **Prep time:** 1 hour

📺 **Season 4, Episode 1**

🔪 **Elimination Challenge:** Reinvent a classic dish against an opponent making the same dish.

ABOUT A TECHNIQUE

smoking gun

Richard B. didn't wait long to show his true colors, using one of his favorite gadgets—his handheld smoker—on *ras el hanout* to heat up classic American crab cakes. The diminutive smoker, which looks like a little drill and runs on batteries, allows chefs to infuse smoke into targeted ingredients without smoking the whole dish.

SERVES 4

FOR THE CRAB CAKES: Using a chefs knife, chop the crab body in large pieces. In a large skillet, heat about 2 tablespoons canola oil over medium-high heat and sauté the crab pieces with the celery salt, fennel seeds, and salt and pepper to taste. Add the water and stir to scrape up the browned bits from the bottom of the pan. Remove from the heat and reserve.

In a small saucepan, heat the apple cider over medium heat and simmer until the cider has reduced to a syrup. Remove from the heat and set aside.

Pick over the lump crabmeat to remove any bits of shell and cartilage and to slightly break up the lumps. Next, crack and pick out the meat from the reserved sautéed crab and combine with the lump crabmeat. In a medium bowl, combine the mayonnaise, onion, chives, and smoke powder. Gently stir in the crabmeat. Season with salt and pepper and *ras el hanout*.

Evenly divide the crab mixture into 4 portions, and form each crab cake using a piece of plastic wrap. Set the cakes aside.

In a large, heavy skillet, melt 2 tablespoons butter and 2 tablespoons canola oil over medium-high heat. Sear the crab cakes until golden on both sides, adding more butter and oil to the pan as needed to prevent sticking. Set aside.

FOR THE BRUSSELS SPROUT SALAD: Trim the stems from the Brussels sprouts. Separate the leaves, reserving all but the smallest leaves.

Bring a pot of water to a boil and have a bowl of ice water ready. Blanch the Brussels sprout leaves. Drain, then shock (see page 15) in the ice bath before draining again. Transfer the leaves to a medium bowl and mix in the mustard-seed pickle and apple. Set aside.

To serve, place a mound of the Brussels sprout salad in the center of each plate and top with a crab cake. Drizzle a little cider syrup over the crab cake.

"Once the smoke blew away, we were left with a wonderful rendition of a crab cake. It showed very forward thinking."

TOM COLICCHIO, **CHEF AND HEAD JUDGE**

Richard Blais, the creative genius of Season 4, and Eli Kirshein, one of the talented Young Turks from Season 6, have a close friendship that dates back to when they worked together at Fishbone and other top restaurants in Atlanta. Eli was a protégé of Richard's and later best man at his wedding. After making his mentor proud with his confident cooking in Season 6, Eli is now behind the stoves in New York City. The impressive work of these two chefs on the show, along with that of Kevin and others, has helped to spotlight Atlanta as a growing culinary mecca.

How would you describe your style of cooking?

ELI: I like to focus on really pristine ingredients, taking something straightforward, easy, and doing something more advanced.

RICHARD: Our style is probably more like a garage band—we go for unique sounds, like when you're playing at low-budget tin-roof places. We're not pristine.

ELI: Of course, he's the king of the metaphor.

RICHARD: We're like Nirvana, mid-'90s.

ELI: And I'm like Radiohead last week.

You worked together at Fishbone. What was that like?

ELI: My mom basically dropped me off in a basket at Richard's doorstep, and he picked me up. I was a kid when I was working at Fishbone.

RICHARD: It was a really big basket. He's twenty-five years old now, and he's still a kid.

ELI: He had me working as garde-manger. Once I sent out burnt shrimp, and I almost saw a vein pop out of his neck.

RICHARD: I almost did check myself into the hospital. I was so mad at him, but that was in the early days. Eli is very much a creative, going above and beyond, and doing what you didn't think

could be done. Every task and challenge I put in front of him, somehow he'd get it done. I'd say, "We've got to make handmade penne for 1,000 people," and he'd say, "That's 12 per plate for 1,000 people" and start doing it. That's testament to his skill level and commitment. He'd never let anything get in the way of his pristine food.

Any other stories of collaborations between the two of you?

RICHARD: Eli helped me with a project in Miami, and we were forced to live together. Eli was sleeping on my couch; he was the first thing I looked at in the morning. The great thing about having Eli live with you is that the living room smells like bacon for a month.

ELI: Richard and his wife have these interesting dietary kicks. They drink diet soda. If I brought home a case of regular Coke it was like the world had ended, since it was taking up space that diet cola could be taking.

I understand you did a little *Top Chef* training together? What did that entail?

ELI: He made me do laps around his restaurant. He told me, "Whatever you do, run everywhere."

RICHARD: Previous to the show he didn't do much running, but anytime you see him on the show, he's running and ahead of the pack. Actually the best advice for me came from Eli. The night before I left for the show, I asked him to talk to me about my food. I was about to pack stuff I didn't typically use or was just experimenting with, and he brought me back to what my food is about.

What is the culinary scene like in Atlanta? Has the show brought more attention to the city?

RICHARD: There are a lot of great restaurants and talented chefs in Atlanta. There's not a ton else to do here except cook great food. Atlanta can compete with any other city in the country. Hopefully my appearance on the show helped scout some great talent, like Eli, Kevin, and Hector.

ELI: Many people are shocked I'm from Atlanta. They're like, "Where's your country accent?" It's a misconception. People from other cities come here to work, but it's not on the résumé. Only in the last year have I embraced it. You should be proud of where you're from culinarily. You should never assume someone is a better cook based on where he or she is from.

What do you admire about each other's food/ craft?

ELI: If I didn't respect his food I wouldn't have worked for him for so long. I'm so enamored of the wit of the food. Every food has a story, a concept, a philosophy behind it. He has an uncanny ability to take the normal and make it funny, inspiring, new. He makes people excited about creative cuisine, and makes it approachable for the masses.

RICHARD: Eli is super-committed and passionate about food. Being around Eli makes you a better chef. He has this contagious passion. And of course I admire his ability to cook and make food tasty. On the show he coined the term "fat kid food," which I think is great. We all get excited about presenting our dishes, but at the end of the day you want to cook something people want to eat.

ANDREW'S SQUID CEVICHE WITH YUZU-MINT GLACIER

YUZU-MINT GLACIER

8 cups water

1½ cups honey or light corn syrup

2 cups *yuzu* juice

1 bunch fresh mint

1 cup agar-agar powder

1 tablespoon salt

SQUID CEVICHE

2 pounds calamari, bodies slit open

2 red onions, finely diced

1 teaspoon red pepper flakes

2 cloves garlic, minced

1 large shallot, finely diced

1 cup raw unsalted macadamia nuts, toasted and chopped

2 cups fresh grapefruit juice

1 cup fresh orange juice

Juice of 1 lime

½ cup sugar

1 tablespoon chopped fresh thyme

¼ cup chopped fresh cilantro

¼ cup chopped fresh mint

1 teaspoon black sesame paste

- -

Soy Tapioca (below)

SERVES 4

FOR THE YUZU GLACIER: In a saucepan, bring the water to a simmer over medium heat. Add the honey and stir to dissolve. Mix in the *yuzu* juice and turn off the heat. Add the mint and let stand to steep for 3 minutes. Stir in the agar-agar until fully dissolved. Strain the liquid, then pour into a wax paper–lined chinois and let set for 3 hours. Once set, turn the chinois over, lift off, and carefully peel away the wax paper to reveal the glacier.

FOR THE SQUID CEVICHE: Preheat a grill to high and lightly oil the grill rack. Have a bowl of ice water ready.

Grill the calamari, turning once, until opaque, about 3 minutes total. Remove from the grill and transfer to a bowl. Nest the bowl in the ice bath to cool. When the calamari is chilled, slice into thin strips.

Combine the onions, red pepper flakes, garlic, shallot, macadamia nuts, citrus juices, and sugar in a large bowl and stir to dissolve the sugar. Cover and refrigerate the ceviche base until chilled.

To serve, toss the calamari with the ceviche base. Divide among 4 plates and sprinkle with the herbs. Spread a drop of the black sesame paste across a small plate with a paintbrush or knife. Spoon the squid mixture alongside the paste. Cut small chunks of the glacier and arrange on the side. Sprinkle the tapioca on top.

🕐 **Prep time:** 1 hour, 30 minutes, plus chilling

🖵 Season 4, Episode 2

🔪 Elimination Challenge: Prepare appetizers based on the diet of a zoo animal—bear, gorilla, lion, penguin,

HOW TO MAKE

soy tapioca

8 cups water

1 cup pearl tapioca

¾ cup soy sauce

¼ cup mushroom soy sauce

1 cup balsamic vinegar

Bring the water to a boil. Add the tapioca and cook until tender but the centers are still white, about 10 minutes. Remove from the heat and drain the tapioca in a sieve. Rinse in cold water for 5 minutes to remove the starch.

In a medium bowl, combine the soy sauce, mushroom soy sauce, and balsamic vinegar. Add the tapioca and soak for at least 2 hours. Drain and use.

ANATOMY OF A WINNING DISH

In the Season 5 finale, Hosea won over the judges with this beautiful and thoughtful dish combining the savory taste of scallops and foie gras with the sweet flavors of *pain perdu*, a New Orleans version of French toast.

1. GARNISH: Micro celery shoots and shredded raw green apple marry well, and finish the dish with a touch of fresh green color and a little crunch.

2. FOAM: Cream is cooked down with star anise, maple syrup, and trim from the foie gras, and just the bubbles are skimmed off to give the essence of those flavors. A touch of soy lecithin keeps the foam light and airy on the plate.

3. FOIE GRAS: The foie gras is seared in a hot pan and then finished with star anise and cinnamon, flavors that are layered throughout the plate.

4. CRUSHED CANDIED PECANS: Pecans roasted with cinnamon, cayenne, and nutmeg are a nod to New Orleans, and add a crunchiness to complement the soft textures of the dish.

5. SCALLOPS: Large U10 sea scallops are just the right size for this dish.

6. APPLE PRESERVES: Green apples—cooked down with cider vinegar, sugar, cinnamon, and peppercorns—add the needed acidity and sharpness to cut against the richness of the rest of the dish.

"I wanted the plate to look stunning, so I made it vertical, with many elements, so you could have a bit of scallop and foie gras on your fork, and then dip it into the apples and nuts to make the perfect bite. I tried to get all the senses involved. You smell the sweet spices, the cinnamon and star anise emanating from the plate. There are different textures; the French toast has a little crispy crust, which is different from the softness of the scallop and foie gras. I also wanted to achieve a balance of tart plus savory plus sweet plus rich."

"It was the best thing I cooked all season."

HOSEA'S SKETCH OF THE WINNING DISH

ANDREW, MARK, AND RICHARD B.'S SALMON WITH "CAVIAR"

WINNER!

MARK'S PARSNIP PURÉE

4 parsnips, peeled and chopped into 1-inch pieces

4 cloves garlic, minced

1 small onion, chopped

1 bay leaf

2 cups heavy cream

1 teaspoon salt, plus more as needed

1/2 teaspoon freshly ground pepper, plus more as needed

1/4 vanilla bean, split lengthwise

ANDREW'S FAUX CAVIAR

3 quarts water

1 cup annatto seeds

One 2.75-ounce box small tapioca pearls

2 cups passion-fruit juice

1 cup canola oil

1 1/2 vanilla beans, split lengthwise

RICHARD'S SALMON

1 1/2 pounds salmon fillet

Salt and freshly ground pepper

4 cups passion-fruit juice

1/2 cup (1 stick) butter

2 fresh passion fruits, quartered

8 ounces watercress, tough stems removed

6 radishes, thinly sliced

SERVES 4

FOR THE PARSNIP PURÉE: In a stockpot over medium-high heat, combine all the ingredients except the vanilla bean. Bring to a simmer and cook until the parsnips are very tender. Drain , reserving the liquid. Discard the bay leaves. Working in batches, transfer the solids to a blender and blend until smooth, adding the reserved liquid as needed. Pass the purée through a fine-mesh sieve into a bowl, tuck in the vanilla bean pieces, and season with salt and pepper to taste.

FOR THE FAUX CAVIAR: In a saucepan over medium-high heat, bring the water to a boil. Add the annatto seeds and cook until the water turns red-orange. Strain through a fine-mesh sieve over a clean, large saucepan. Place over medium-high heat and return the water to a boil. Add the tapioca and cook until translucent, about 15 minutes.

In another saucepan over medium-high heat, simmer the passion-fruit juice until reduced by one-fourth. Have a bowl of ice-water ready.

Drain the tapioca and add it to the fruit- juice reduction. Remove the pan from the heat, and nest it in the ice-water bath. Stir to cool down the tapioca, then refrigerate.

CONTINUED

🕐 **Prep time:** 1 hour, 30 minutes

🖵 **Season 4, Episode 4**

🔪 **Elimination Challenge:**
Create a dish inspired by your favorite film. (In this case, *Willy Wonka and the Chocolate Factory*.)

ABOUT AN INGREDIENT

annatto

Annatto seeds are traditionally used in Latin American and Caribbean cuisine for both the flavor and the bright orange color they impart. Recently, they have become popular in Asian cooking. The advantage of annatto is that while it dyes other foods, it has a very mild flavor. It is used in commercial foods to color everything from butter to boxed mac and cheese. Andrew, Mark, and Richard B. used annatto to make trompe l'oeil caviar out of regular tapioca balls.

In a saucepan, heat the oil over low heat. Scrape seeds from the vanilla beans into the oil and then and then add the beans to the oil. Let stand to allow the vanilla to infuse the oil and let the oil cool to room temperature, about 30 minutes.

Once cooled, pour the infused oil over the fruit tapioca and allow it to settle on the top (do not mix it in). Just before serving, drain about half of the oil from the top, then stir until the remaining oil is well combined and the mixture has emulsified.

FOR THE SALMON: Fill a pot three-fourths full of water and heat until it registers 120°F on a deep-frying or candy thermometer. Maintain the temperature by keeping the heat on low or periodically turning the burner off and on.

Season the salmon with salt and pepper, place in a large, heavy-duty lock-top bag, and add 2 cups of the passion fruit juice and 3 to 4 tablespoons of the butter. Seal the bag, squeezing out as much air as possible. Put the bag in the hot water and cook until opaque, 7 to 8 minutes. Remove the salmon from the water bath and set aside.

Meanwhile, combine the remaining 2 cups passion-fruit juice with the passion fruits in a saucepan over medium-high heat and reduce by one-third. Remove from the heat and finish the sauce with the remaining 4 to 5 tablespoons butter. Set aside.

To serve, in a bowl, toss together the watercress and radishes. Cut the salmon into serving pieces.

Spoon a portion of the parsnip purée in the center of each plate. Top each with a piece of salmon. Pour a little passion-fruit sauce over the fish. Arrange the watercress salad on the side and spoon some of the faux caviar on top of the salad.

> "Molecular gastronomy is not whiz-bang gadget gizmo. It's the basis to take traditional items and, because of science, make them better."
>
> RICHARD B., SEASON 4

Q + A

marcel

This rapping, foam-making maestro of Season 2 just barely lost out to Ilan in a very closely fought finale. Marcel didn't invent gelées or many of the intriguing concoctions he prepared on the show, but he introduced these things to a wider audience and also embodied the kind of creative experimentation that is so important for a modern cook. Marcel continues to make his name as an avant-garde chef.

How would you describe your style of cooking?

I work with avant-garde cuisine. I'd call it modern global with a foundation rooted in the classics. I update and renovate classic dishes. For example, tempura batter is classic, but I make it in a blender, and then I put it through a siphon and charge it with soda. It's the lightest, whitest, crispiest tempura you'll ever taste. It's based on technique, but I've made it better with technology.

What are your thoughts on molecular gastronomy?

All cooking is molecular if you look at it on a scientific level. Every time you heat something up you are changing the molecular structure of the food. It's all science, when any phenomenon happens within the ingredients. Molecular gastronomy refers to the science behind cooking, but there's a science behind all cooking.

Are you still making foams?

I did a tasting menu in Tokyo, and people were disappointed that I didn't use foam. I'm refining and showing my strength, trying not to use foams and airs in everything I do. Foams are a beautiful way to exhibit a flavor, and there are a lot of applications and appropriate uses for them. But there is a time and a place.

What is one of your signature techniques?

I have a whole archive and collection of techniques that I've been refining over the course of my culinary extravaganza. I've perfected the microwave siphon cake. It's like a sponge cake. You can use

a nut butter, praline, pine nuts, or vegetable purées. You make a cake batter in a blender. You shoot it into plastic cups, filling them one-third full. Then you nuke it 45 seconds at 900 watts and it quadruples in volume. It has an airy, spongy soufflé texture.

What are the most common mistakes people make when cooking at home?

People don't talk to their food. If you're searing a scallop, talk to a scallop. Like, "Scallop, are you ready for me to flip you over?" The food will tell you how to cook it. I talk to ingredients. People don't give enough love and respect to the ingredients.

What is your least favorite ingredient?

I don't like green bell peppers—they're unfit for human consumption. There's this bell pepper craze, and a lot of people use them for color, even though they don't go with the dish. It's not that I hate the bell pepper. It just overpowers every other flavor. I can't stand inappropriate use of ingredients.

Have you made any culinary blunders?

When I was practicing for the *Top Chef* finale, I taught myself to make the isomalt bonbons. You have to heat the sugar to 500 degrees, and I totally burnt my thumb. Anytime you're developing new techniques, you're going to make mistakes.

MARCEL'S CHERRY TART AND FOAM

1 sheet puff pastry

5 cups cherries, stemmed

4 cups cherry juice

Honey

Cherry Gelée (below)

Four 3.8 ounce bars 70 percent cacao chocolate

2 cups heavy cream

Sugar

1 teaspoon lecithin

MAKES TEN 3-INCH TARTS

Preheat the oven to 350°F.

Lay the puff pastry out on a floured surface and cut out ten 3-inch rounds. Transfer the pastry rounds to a baking sheet lined with a Silpat or parchment paper and weight down each round with a couple of pastry weights in the center. Bake in the oven for 10 to 15 minutes.

Pit 50 of the cherries and slice in half. Set aside.

Pit the remaining cherries. In a medium saucepan, combine the cherries with 2 cups of the cherry juice and a little honey to taste over medium heat. Bring to a simmer and cook until the cherries are soft, about 15 minutes. Remove from the heat and, with a slotted spoon, transfer the cherries to a food processor and purée until smooth. Press through a fine-mesh sieve. Set the purée aside.

Remove the Cherry Gelée from the mold and set aside.

Melt the chocolate in the top of a double boiler and whisk in 1 cup of the cream and sugar to taste. Remove from the heat and set aside. With an electric mixer, whip the remaining 1 cup cream to medium peaks. Transfer the cream a pastry bag fitted with a medium tip or a plastic bag with the corner snipped off.

Arrange the halved cherries on the puff pastry rounds and spoon some of the purée over each, dividing evenly. Pipe the whipped cream on top of the cherries. Set aside.

Combine the remaining 2 cups cherry juice with the lecithin in a medium bowl and foam the mixture using an immersion blender.

To serve, place a tart on a dessert plate, spoon the cherry foam on top of the tart, drizzle with chocolate, and serve with a slice of cherry gelée on the side.

⏱ **Prep time:** 2 hours, including chilling

🖥 Season 2, Episode 9

✒ Elimination Challenge:
Create a dish based on one of the seven deadly sins.

HOW TO MAKE

cherry gelée

2 cups cherry juice
2 tablespoons powdered gelatin

In a saucepan, bring the cherry juice to a simmer, then remove from the heat. Put the gelatin powder in a bowl, add 1 cup of the hot cherry juice and stir until the gelatin is dissolved. Pour the gelatin mixture back into the saucepan and stir to combine. Transfer the cherry gelatin to a small baking dish and refrigerate until set, about 2 hours.

RESTAURANT WARS

One of the most anticipated and dreaded challenges every season, Restaurant Wars pits two teams against each other to open a restaurant, complete with theme, name, cohesive menu, and even décor—all in 24 hours. This all-out competition has brought out the best and worst in participants; many a talented chef'testant has gone down for failing in the role of executive chef, while others have truly shined and shown us what they are capable of under mad pressure and time constraints. Here are some of the restaurant concepts and menus from past seasons.

SEASON 4

WINNER!

Restaurant: Warehouse Kitchen
MEMBERS: Antonia, Nikki, Richard B., Stephanie
CONCEPT: New American Gastro-Pub

Menu:
Beet and Goat Cheese Salad with *Ras el Hanout*
Linguine with Clams
Trout with Cauliflower and Hazelnut Brown Butter
Lamb Two Ways
Gorgonzola Cheesecake (page 203)
Banana Scallops

Restaurant: Mai Buddha
MEMBERS: Dale T., Lisa, Jennifer B., Spike
CONCEPT: Pan-Asian

Menu:
Shrimp Laksa
Pork and Pickled-Plum Pot Stickers
Butterscotch Miso Scallops
Braised Short Ribs
Halo-Halo
Mango Sticky Rice

SEASON 5

Restaurant: Sahana
MEMBERS: Carla, Jamie, Jeff, Radhika
CONCEPT: Indian Middle-Eastern Spice Route

Menu:
Curried Carrot Soup with Paprika Oil and Raita
Grilled Scallop with Chickpea Cake
Cinnamon and Saffron–Braised Lamb Shank
White Lentil Tabbouli with Seared Snapper
Spiced Chocolate Cake with Cashew Brittle
Frozen Yogurt

WINNER!

Restaurant: Sunset Lounge
MEMBERS: Fabio, Hosea, Leah, Stefan
CONCEPT: Asian-Inspired

Menu:
Sashimi Two Ways & Curry Seafood Bisque
Braised Boneless Beef Short Ribs
Coconut-Curry Bisque
Seared Black Cod with Chili Sauce
Orange Chocolate Rice Parfait & Assorted "Lollipops"
Ginger-Lemongrass Panna Cotta (page 184)

SEASON 6

WINNER!

Restaurant: REVolt
MEMBERS: Bryan, Eli, Michael V., Robin
CONCEPT: Modern American

Menu:
Smoked Arctic Char with Beet Sauce and Horseradish Cream
Chicken and Calamari Pasta
Duo of Beef, Braised Short Ribs
Cod with Mussel Billi Bi
Chocolate Ganache with Spearmint Ice Cream
Pear Pithivier

Restaurant: Mission
MEMBERS: Jennifer C., Kevin, Laurine, Mike,
CONCEPT: Modern American

Menu:
Asparagus and Six-Minute Egg
Arctic Char Tartare
Trout with Hazelnut Butter
Bouillabaisse
Lamb with Carrot Jam
Pork Three Ways

TOP CHEF MASTERS BIOS

Top Chef Masters Season 1 pitted 24 world-renowned chefs against each other. Here's a spotlight on some of the master chefs.

RICK BAYLESS

Through his award-winning cookbooks, long-running TV program, and mini-empire of restaurants in the heart of Chicago, Rick Bayless has done more than any other American chef to expand understanding of, and appreciation for, authentic Mexican cuisine. He exuded a calm confidence during the entire season, and in the final dinner his elegant, flavorful procession from the Oklahoma barbecue of his youth to the modern Mexican dishes of today earned him the title of Top Chef Master.

WINNER!

Finale Menu
Barbecued Quail with Hickory House Sauce, Sour Slaw, and Watermelon Salad

Seared Ahi Tuna over Oaxacan Black Mole with Braised Chicken, Plantain Tamales, and Grilled Nopales

Achiote-Marinated Cochinta Pibil with Sunchoke Purée, Crispy Pigs' Feet, and Pickled Red Onion

Arroz a la Tumbada with Tomato-Jalapeño Broth and Chorizo Air

MICHAEL CHIARELLO

Michael Chiarello has starred in his own cooking show, written cookbooks, and even operates a winery. He is as comfortable behind a stove as in front of the camera. His latest venture, Bottega Restaurant in the Napa Valley, features his trademark rustic-yet-sophisticated Italian cuisine. On *Top Chef Masters,* his creamy polenta and tender braised short ribs nearly stole the show.

Finale Menu
Crispy Potato Gnocchi with Black Truffle and Taleggio Fonduta and Ricotta Gnocchi with Old Hen Tomato Sauce

Ancient Grain Polenta with Wild Mushroom and Balsamic Rabbit Ragu, Asparagus and Grilled Rabbit Liver

Ginger Stuffed Rouget with Mango Salad, Fresh Wasabi, and Bottarga

Brined Short Ribs with Five-Onion Cavalo Nero and Essence of Smoldering Vines

HUBERT KELLER

Chef-owner of Fleur de Lys and the casual Burger Bar (both with locations in San Francisco and Las Vegas), Keller is one of the country's finest chefs. A consummate professional who thinks on his feet, on *Top Chef Masters* Hubert proved he's as comfortable draining pasta in a dorm bathroom as he is producing dishes inspired by his Alsatian childhood.

Finale Menu
Baekeoffe: Alsatian Lamb, Beef, Pork, and Potato Stew

Salmon Soufflé with Royal Osetra Caviar and Riesling Sauce, Choucroute Flan

Lamb Chop with Vegetable Mousseline, Blanched Garlic, and Vanilla-Merlot Sauce

Wagyú Beef Cheeks and Celery Purée with Pinot Noir, Lemongrass, and Ginger Sauce

ANITA LO

Chef-owner of Annisa in New York's Greenwich Village, Anita Lo blends Southeast Asian flavors with classic French techniques she learned working in the best restaurants in Paris. In the Magic Castle Challenge she served up a mind-boggling daikon radish stuffed with steak tartare, disguised as a stuffed scallop.

ART SMITH

In ten years as Oprah Winfrey's private chef, Art Smith has become known as much for his warm personality as his Southern comfort food. Equal parts chef, celebrity, and humanitarian, Art is chef-owner of multiple restaurants, and has established the non-profit organization Common Threads.

SUZANNE TRACHT

Suzanne Tracht worked her way up through some of Los Angeles' hottest kitchens—including Campanile and Jozu—before opening Jar, the modern steakhouse where she is owner and chef. Cool and unflappable, Suzanne's multifaceted plate featuring Risotto with Uni (page 92) for the Lost Supper Challenge landed her a spot in the Champions round.

WYLIE DUFRESNE

The creative force behind New York's Michelin star–bearing wd~50, Wylie Dufresne is a pioneer of the molecular gastronomy/creative cooking movement. On *Top Chef Masters*, Wylie thrilled the judges with his elegantly squared-off roast chicken and slow-poached egg, but fell just behind Suzanne Tracht to miss out on the Champions round.

JOHN BESH

Chef-owner of August and several other top eateries in New Orleans, John Besh combines his classic French training with a modern take on Creole cooking. At the Magic Castle challenge on *Top Chef Masters*, John really got into the spirit, using liquid nitrogen to add some zippy showmanship to his dish

RICK MOONEN

Awarded three stars from the *New York Times*, Rick Moonen has established an empire based on sustainable seafood. His bilevel restaurant RM in the Mandalay Bay, Las Vegas, was the backdrop for Season 6 Restaurant Wars. A man of prodigious energy, on *Top Chef Masters* he served opaka-paka and barramundi ceviche to the masses.

LAST COURSE: THE ART OF DESSERT

187

203

189

195

207

STEFAN'S GINGER-LEMONGRASS PANNA COTTA

4 cups heavy cream

2 sheets leaf gelatin,
or 1/2 teaspoon powdered gelatin

1/4 cup sugar

1 teaspoon ground turmeric

5-inch piece fresh ginger, peeled
and sliced into thin coins

1-inch piece fresh ginger, grated,
pulp squeezed and juices reserved

10 stalks lemongrass, tender bottom
parts only, halved and crushed

1/3 cup honey, preferably wildflower

1 ripe peach, pitted, peeled, and
cut into thin slices

5 fresh mint sprigs

🕐 **Prep time:** 1 hour,
plus chilling

🖵 Season 5, Episode 9

✎ **Elimination Challenge:**
Restaurant Wars. Open a restaurant for
dinner service.

ABOUT AN INGREDIENT

gelatin

Gelatin, which is extracted from animal
collagen, has the ability to transform a
liquid into a solid when it is heated and
then cooled. One of the favorite uses for
gelatin is *panna cotta*. Just cream cooked
with gelatin and sugar, *panna cotta* is
one of the simplest of desserts and can
be used as a blank canvas on which to
feature any combination of ingredients.

SERVES 5

In a large saucepan over medium heat, warm the cream until it bubbles. Add the gelatin and sugar and cook, stirring, until dissolved. Transfer half of the cream mixture to another pan over medium heat. Add the ginger coins, ginger pulp, and turmeric to the first pan; and add the lemongrass to the second. Bring both mixtures to a boil, remove from the heat, and set aside to steep for 20 minutes, stirring occasionally to keep a skin from forming. Strain, keeping each cream separate. Discard the solids.

Divide the ginger-turmeric cream among five 1-cup ramekins, filling them slightly less than halfway. Refrigerate until firm, about 2 hours. Top the first layer with a layer of lemongrass cream. Chill again for at least 2 hours or up to overnight.

In a small saucepan over low heat, warm the honey. Add the reserved ginger juices to the warm honey. Mix well and remove from the heat to cool.

To serve, unmold each *panna cotta* to an individual dessert plate. Drizzle with a little ginger honey and garnish with the peach slices and mint.

> "Thank God I made two desserts, and the judges were happy. It would be my worst nightmare to be on the losing team of Restaurant Wars."
>
> STEFAN, SEASON 5

RICK MOONEN'S LEMON CUSTARD WITH PINEAPPLE EMULSION

LEMON CUSTARD

1/2 cup cold buttermilk

1 sheet leaf gelatin,
or 1 teaspoon powdered gelatin

1 cup heavy cream

1/2 cup sugar

Pinch of salt

1/2 vanilla bean, split lengthwise

1/2 lemon

1 tablespoon diced preserved
lemon rind or candied lemon rind

GINGERSNAP TOPPING

6 gingersnaps

1 tablespoon macadamia nuts, toasted

1/4 cup shredded coconut, toasted

PINEAPPLE EMULSION

1/2 ripe pineapple, peeled and
cut into large chunks

Grated zest and juice of 1 lime

1/2 vanilla bean, split lengthwise

SERVES 6

FOR THE LEMON CUSTARD: Put the cold buttermilk in a medium bowl and add the gelatin to soften. In a large saucepan, combine the cream, sugar, salt, and vanilla beans over medium-low heat. Whisk the cream as it heats up to release the vanilla bean flavor. When the cream begins to simmer, squeeze the lemon half into the cream and carefully strain the hot liquid into the bowl of buttermilk and gelatin. Whisk to dissolve the gelatin. Divide the lemon custard among six 1-cup ramekins and sprinkle the lemon rind over the top. Refrigerate until the custard is set, at least 2 hours.

FOR THE GINGERSNAP TOPPING: Combine the gingersnaps, macadamia nuts, and coconut in a food processor and pulse into medium crumbs. Set aside.

FOR THE PINEAPPLE EMULSION: In a blender, combine the pineapple, a splash of water, and the lime zest and juice. Scrape in the seeds from the vanilla bean pieces and discard the bean. Blend until smooth, then strain the emulsion through a fine-mesh sieve. Set aside.

To serve, unmold the lemon custards onto individual dessert plates. Generously top with an even coating of the gingersnap topping. Spoon a small amount of the pineapple emulsion over the top.

🕐 **Prep time:** 45 minutes, plus cooling

📺 *Top Chef Masters,*
Season 1, Episode 5

🔪 **Elimination Challenge:**
Create a mini appetizer, entrée, and dessert for 100 people.

> "This silky custard is ree-di-cu-lous. Knock-out delicious."

KELLY CHOI, *TOP CHEF MASTERS* HOST

JEFF'S LAVENDER CRÈME BRÛLÉE

4 cups heavy cream

1 vanilla bean, split lengthwise

12 to 16 fresh lavender flowers

10 egg yolks

1/2 cup sugar, plus 6 tablespoons

Mixed berries such as blueberries, blackberries, and raspberries for serving

Fresh mint sprigs for garnish

SERVES 6

Preheat the oven to 300°F.

In a medium saucepan, bring the cream to a gentle simmer over medium heat. Remove from the heat and scrape in the seeds from the vanilla bean. Add the bean pieces and the lavender. Cover and steep the flavorings in the cream for 15 minutes, then strain through a fine-mesh sieve into a clean saucepan.

In a medium bowl or stand mixer, whisk the egg yolks with the 1/2 cup sugar until frothy. Temper the yolks by adding about 1/2 cup of the heated cream to the bowl while whisking constantly to prevent curdling. Dribble another 1/2 cup cream into the bowl, whisking until well combined. Pour the warmed egg mixture into the saucepan of cream and heat slowly over low heat, stirring constantly, until the custard is slightly thick and coats a spoon, about 15 minutes.

Divide the custard among six 1-cup ramekins and place the ramekins in a large baking pan. Add 1 inch of hot water to the pan, cover the custards with aluminum foil, and bake until the custards are just set and still jiggly in the center, about 40 minutes.

Remove the ramekins from the water bath, let cool on a wire rack, then transfer to the refrigerator to chill, at least 2 hours.

To serve, sprinkle 1 tablespoon sugar over each ramekin. Moving a kitchen blowtorch from side to side, heat the sugar until it melts and caramelizes into a brittle, golden brown topping. Garnish each crème brûlée with a spoonful of berries and sprig of fresh mint.

🕐 **Prep time:** 1 hour, 30 minutes

🖥 **Season 5, Episode 8**

🔪 **Elimination Challenge:** Create a seasonal lunch using fresh ingredients from a farm.

ABOUT A TECHNIQUE

torching it

It wouldn't be a brûlée without the burnt sugar crust. The best part of this sinful French custard is the top, which is sprinkled with sugar and then burnt with a mini blowtorch, or else placed under the broiler, to create the dish's signature caramelization. The glassine exterior is then cracked with a spoon before devouring.

MICHAEL V.'S APPLE SORBET

GOAT CHEESE COOKIE

1 cup fresh goat cheese, softened

1 cup sugar

1 cup all-purpose flour

3 egg whites

Sea salt and freshly ground pepper

APPLE SORBET

4 cups fresh apple juice

1 vanilla bean, split lengthwise

2 cinnamon sticks

2 star anise pods

2 allspice berries

2 Granny Smith apples, peeled and cut into thin slices

1/2 cup water (optional)

1/2 teaspoon xanthan gum

1/4 cup fresh lemon juice

1/2 cup Goldschläger

1/2 cup rum

Fresh dill sprigs for garnish

Shredded lemon zest for garnish

SERVES 4

FOR THE GOAT CHEESE COOKIE: Preheat the oven to 350°F.

In a bowl, using an electric mixer, beat together the goat cheese and sugar until smooth. Mix in the flour and egg whites with a spatula. Spread the mixture on a Silpat- or parchment-lined baking sheet and season with salt and pepper. Bake until golden brown, about 10 to 12 minutes.

FOR THE APPLE SORBET: In a large saucepan, bring the apple juice to a simmer over medium-high heat. Reduce the heat to low and scrape in the seeds of the vanilla bean, then add the bean, the cinnamon stick, star anise, and allspice berries, and simmer for 30 minutes.

Place the apple slices in a microwave-safe bowl and cover with plastic wrap. Microwave on high until tender, about 3 minutes. Alternatively, in a sauté pan, cook the apple slices with the water over medium heat until tender, about 8 minutes.

Strain the apple juice into a blender. Add the apple slices and xanthan gum. Blend on medium speed until perfectly smooth and emulsified. Pour the mixture into a container and let cool. Once cool, add the lemon juice, Goldschläger, and rum. Freeze in an ice-cream maker according to the manufacturer's instructions.

To serve, scoop the sorbet into glasses. Garnish each glass with a goat cheese cookie, a fresh dill sprig, and lemon zest.

Prep time: 1 hour, plus chilling

Season 6, Episode 2

Elimination Challenge:
Cater a bachelor/bachelorette party in two teams split by gender.

ABOUT AN INGREDIENT

xanthan gum

Xanthan gum was first introduced to viewers as part of Marcel's bag of tricks on Season 2 and is now a standard item in the *Top Chef* pantry. Useful for making thickened jams and jellies, xanthan gum is a thickener that, unlike gelatin, stabilizes liquids at any temperature, allowing chefs to try all kinds of fun things. You will also find it's used as a thickener in thousands of commercial products, from salad dressings to yogurt.

CARLA'S PASTRY DEMO

Carla Hall won over Season 5 viewers with her warm and kooky personality. One of the few chef'testants who felt comfortable making desserts, she was pegged as the show pastry chef. Between "sending the love" from the kitchen and teaching the world a new call-and-response ("Hootie-Hoo!"), Carla crept up on the competition and made it all the way to the finale in New Orleans.

CARLA'S VERSATILE TART PASTRY

Some of Carla's best moments on the show involved pastry, including her Nectarine and Strawberry Tartlets (page 195). Her distinctive method for making pastry is inspired by cook-book author Shirley Corriher. A stand mixer is ideal for this technique, but you can also use a food processor, so long as you are careful not to overprocess the dough.

1. Add 1 tablespoon sugar and 1 teaspoon salt to 1/3 cup cold water and stir to dissolve. Place in the fridge until ready to use.

2. Cut 1 cup (2 sticks) unsalted butter into small, even cubes.

3. Put 2 cups all-purpose flour in the bowl of a stand mixer, then toss the butter cubes one by one into the flour so they are lightly coated and separate.

4. Mix the flour and butter on low speed just until the butter pieces are broken down to the size of small peas, about 30 seconds.

5. While the mixer is running, add the sugar-salt water all at once and beat until the dough just comes together—about 30 seconds longer. Turn off the mixer.

6. Form the dough into 2 disks, each about 3/4 inch thick and wrap them in plastic wrap. Chill for at least 30 minutes.

7. Roll a disk out about 1/8 inch thick, place it in the tart pan, trim it, and return it to the fridge or freezer briefly before baking.

"I send out some love with the food I cook."

ON HER SIGNATURE STYLE: Upscale comfort food with a touch of French influence.

ON MINDFULNESS: Be present—you need to look for visual cues when you're cooking, and not just follow directions blindly.

FIVE FAVORITE TARTS

- Rustic, free-form apple tart

- Layering of fruit torte with crumble on top

- Peach or nectarine cobbler

- Savory tomato custard with rata-touille (using a Parmesan crust)

- Goat cheese tartlets

DESSERT DISASTERS

The most dreaded words in the *Top Chef* lexicon? Dessert Challenge. Season after season we've watched the chefs strain to make something sweet, and with good reason: desserts have been the not-so-sweet end for plenty of contestants. Add too much sugar? Soufflé fail to rise? Don't know how to make a wedding cake in 24 hours? Tough luck.

No More S'Mores:
Season 5, Episode 3
Richard S. decided to combine two of the Foo Fighters's favorites—bananas and s'mores—but his topping ended up looking like "spit on the plate."

Failure to Set:
Season 5, Episode 4
After Alex's rose-infused crème brûlée did not set in time for the *Today* show demo, he was promptly sent home.

Whipped:
Season 5, Episode 7
For her dessert, Ariane overwhipped her cream, nearly turning it to butter. French pastry chef Jean-Christophe Novelli was so unimpressed that he declined to even taste it.

Say No to 1980s Desserts:
Season 5, Finale
Despite being the frontrunner going into the finale, Stefan made a misstep with his final dessert course, which may have cost him the title.

Creamed:
Top Chef Masters
Season 1, Episode 8
Although his almond brittle was tasty, Art Smith was eliminated for using store-bought rice ice cream.

Childs Play:
Season 6, Episode 11
Robin was sent home for her Panna Cotta, inspired by stained glass. Guest judge Nigella Lawson pronounced the dessert "child's play."

ROBIN'S APPLE CRISP AND FRUIT MÊLÉE

APPLE CRISP TOPPING

1/2 cup unsalted butter

1 cup rolled oats

1 teaspoon ground cinnamon

1/2 teaspoon ground ginger

1/4 teaspoon ground cardamom

1/4 teaspoon Chinese
five-spice powder

1/2 teaspoon minced orange zest

1/3 to 1/2 cup all-purpose flour

APPLE CRISP FILLING

Vegetable oil spray

4 large apples, peeled, cored, and
cut into 1/8-inch-thick slices

1 tablespoon fresh lemon juice

1/2 cup sugar

1 teaspoon ground cinnamon

1/2 teaspoon ground allspice

1/2 teaspoon ground ginger

1/3 cup all-purpose flour,
or as needed

CARDAMOM WHIPPED CREAM

2 cups heavy cream

1 to 2 tablespoons sugar

1/2 teaspoon ground cardamom

RAW SALAD

1 fennel bulb, trimmed, cored, and
cut into 1/4-inch dice, fronds reserved

2 apples, cored and cut into
1/4-inch dice

1/2 cup green seedless grapes,
quartered

1/2 cup red seedless grapes,
quartered

1 teaspoon finely minced shallot

1/4 cup slivered almonds

1/4 cup dried cranberries

Juice of 1/2 lemon

GINGER VINAIGRETTE

1-inch piece fresh ginger, peeled
and smashed

Juice of 1/2 lemon

1 cup water

1/2 cup rice vinegar

1/4 cup sugar

1 teaspoon dry mustard

1/2 cup grapeseed oil

Sea salt and freshly ground pepper

Honey

Amaretto Caramel Sauce (facing page)

Prep time: 1 hour, 45 minutes

Season 6, Episode 6

Quickfire Challenge:
Create a dish inspired by the angel
and the devil on your shoulder.

SERVES 10 TO 12

FOR THE APPLE CRISP TOPPING: In a medium bowl, beat together the butter, oats, cinnamon, ginger, cardamom, five-spice powder, and zest. Mixing by hand, incorporate enough flour to make the mixture dry and crumbly. Set aside.

FOR THE APPLE CRISP FILLING: Preheat the oven to 375°F.

Lightly coat a 9-by-13 baking dish with cooking spray. In a large bowl, mix together the apples, lemon juice, sugar, cinnamon, allspice, and ginger. Add just enough of the flour to bind the ingredients together (the consistency should not be dry). Transfer the filling to the prepared baking dish and sprinkle evenly with the crisp topping. Bake until bubbly and golden brown, about 1 hour. While the crisp is baking, make the whipped cream, salad, and vinaigrette.

FOR THE CARDAMOM WHIPPED CREAM: In a large chilled bowl, beat the cream with an electric mixer. As the cream begins to thicken, sprinkle in sugar to taste and the cardamom. Continue to whip the cream until light, stiff peaks form. Cover and refrigerate until ready to serve.

FOR THE RAW SALAD: Chop the reserved fennel fronds. In a medium bowl, combine the fronds with the diced fennel, apples, grapes, shallot, almonds, and cranberries. Toss with the lemon juice until well combined. Set aside.

FOR THE GINGER VINAIGRETTE: In a medium bowl, whisk together the ginger, lemon, water, vinegar, sugar, and mustard. While whisking constantly, slowly stream in the oil until the vinaigrette is emulsified. Season with salt, pepper, and honey to taste.

To serve, dress the salad with the ginger vinaigrette. Drizzle one side of each dessert plate with the Amaretto Caramel Sauce and place a portion of the apple crisp on top. Place a dollop of the cardamom whipped cream on the crisp. Alternatively, place an individual dish on one side of each dessert plate, top with a dollop of the cream, and drizzle with the sauce. Spoon a serving of the raw salad on the side.

HOW TO MAKE

amaretto caramel sauce

1 cup sugar
2 tablespoons light corn syrup
1 tablespoon fresh lemon juice
2 tablespoons water
2 tablespoons cold unsalted butter, minced
$1/4$ cup heavy cream
1 to 2 tablespoons amaretto
Pinch of salt
Pinch of ground cardamom

In a small saucepan, combine the sugar, corn syrup, lemon juice, and water over medium heat and bring to a gentle boil. Cook, without stirring, until the syrup turns a deep amber, about 20 minutes. Remove from the heat. Whisk in the butter and cream (careful: it may spatter and hiss). Finish with amaretto to taste, salt, and cardamom.

"Most people think apple crisp would be so simple, but you executed it really well."

MICHELLE BERNSTEIN,
CHEF AND GUEST JUDGE

CARLA'S NECTARINE AND STRAWBERRY TARTLETS

NECTARINE AND STRAWBERRY FILLING

2 teaspoons canola oil

10 nectarines, peeled and cut into ½-inch chunks

2 tablespoons unsalted butter

1 cup sour plums, peeled and pitted

1 cup sour cherries, pitted

3 sprigs fresh thyme

½ cup firmly packed brown sugar, or as needed

¼ teaspoon salt

¼ cup water

2 tablespoons cornstarch

2 teaspoons vanilla extract

2 pints strawberries, hulled and quartered

SWEET LEMON-THYME CREAM

1 cup heavy cream

¼ cup *fromage blanc*

¼ cup plain whole-milk yogurt

3 tablespoons granulated sugar, or as needed

2 teaspoons grated lemon zest

1 teaspoon finely chopped fresh thyme

Carla's Versatile Tart Pastry (page 190)

2 eggs combined with 1 tablespoon water for an egg wash

2 tablespoons granulated sugar

MAKES 8 TARTLETS

FOR THE FILLING: In a large, heavy-bottomed skillet, heat the canola oil over medium-high heat. Quickly sear the nectarines. Add the butter, then stir in the plums, cherries, thyme sprigs, brown sugar, and salt. In a small bowl, stir together the water, cornstarch, and vanilla. Immediately pour the cornstarch mixture into the fruit and stir. Bring to a boil to cook down the cornstarch. Taste for sweetness and adjust with brown sugar, if needed. Remove from the heat. Stir in the strawberries and let cool.

FOR THE LEMON-THYME CREAM: While the filling cools, with a whisk or mixer, whip the cream to soft peaks. Using a spatula, fold in the *fromage blanc* and yogurt. Add the sugar, lemon zest, and thyme. Taste for sweetness and adjust if necessary. Cover and chill in the refrigerator.

Preheat the oven to 375°F. Divide each dough disk into 4 equal pieces.

On a lightly floured work surface, roll out each pastry portion into a 6-inch round. Spoon some filling in the center of each round, leaving a 1½-inch border. Pleat and fold the pastry around the filling. Brush the pastry with the egg wash and sprinkle with the sugar. Using a spatula, transfer the tartlets to a baking dish. Bake until golden brown and bubbly, about 18 minutes.

To serve, spoon a dollop of the lemon-thyme cream on each tartlet.

 Prep time: 2 hours

Season 5, Episode 8

Elimination Challenge: Create a seasonal lunch using fresh ingredients from a farm.

Q + A

anita lo and suzanne tracht

Some of the best restaurants in the country are run by women chefs. Yet even today it's challenging to get ahead as a woman in the professional kitchen, where the pace is breakneck, the hours grueling, and the ambience often one of a sports-team locker room. Award-winning chefs like Anita Lo and Suzanne Tracht are proving that women can rise to the very top of this profession, and do it on their own terms.

Tracht, the chef-owner of Jar steakhouse in West Los Angeles, made it to the finals of *Top Chef Masters*, and won over the judges in the *Lost* Elimination with her mixed plate, which included Risotto with Uni (page 92). Lo, who trained in France and is chef-owner of Annisa in Greenwich Village, wowed the *Top Chef Masters* judges and fellow chefs with her creative and flavorful creations, including her Soft-Scrambled Egg with Shiitakes served in an eggshell (page 133).

What was your experience on *Top Chef Masters* like?

SUZANNE: I had a great experience. When they said it was for charity, there wasn't any thinking about it. The best part was networking with other chefs and getting out of the same day-to-day and into a new kitchen.

ANITA: It was wonderful to be with all the really amazing chefs. It was also a little harrowing. It's not the way we normally cook. My kitchen is a much more controlled environment where we can make sure everything is perfect.

How did it feel to be one of the last women standing?

ANITA: I'm so used to being one of the only women in the kitchen; this industry does tend to be male-dominated.

SUZANNE: It felt really good. I wanted to make it further. I got kicked off for a dumb grouper thing. But I was happy to get back to my normal life.

What challenges do women face in the kitchen?

SUZANNE: We all face the same challenge: to be on top of your game. You have to know what's going on, what people like, what's in season. We all have to work our way up, which takes a lot of years and experience. You never stop learning.

ANITA: Women haven't been raised to go after their careers. They've been raised to look at their life holistically, whereas men have been raised to look at career first. The successful women that I know that own their own restaurants have "house husbands," which is not traditional, or they can afford a nanny.

SUZANNE: It's a hard profession, especially if you want to start a family. I have two teenagers, and once they became teenagers, I realized that I had to show them that I wasn't off playing, that I was doing something that I love to do.

Who are the most influential women cooking today?

SUZANNE: Nancy Silverton, Emily Luchetti, Suzanne Goin, Cindy Pawlcyn.

"Suzanne is fabulous. She is so dry; I love hanging out with her."

ANITA LO

"I loved working with Anita. I respect her style and her food; she knows her stuff."

SUZANNE TRACHT

ANITA: Alice Waters has clearly influenced the world. And also Anne-Sophie Pic in France, Rose Gray and Ruth Rogers from the River Cafe in London, and Martha Stewart.

Is it important to you to be a role model for women chefs?

ANITA: Definitely. I have had a lot of women come to my kitchen, and I hope to see them succeed. Several of them have gone off to own their own restaurants, which makes me very proud.

SUZANNE: Absolutely. And to be a role model for chefs in general.

What advice do you have for women cooks?

SUZANNE: Have skin like an alligator and stay focused. Women make great leaders in the kitchen because they have good taste and good sense, and are caring, which is important because a kitchen is a family. You're only as good as the people who surround you.

ANITA: Do what you love and don't be afraid to put what you want first.

DANNY'S POUND CAKE
WITH STRAWBERRY-LEMON COMPOTE

POUND CAKE

1½ pounds (6 sticks) butter, at room temperature, plus more for pan

4½ cups all-purpose flour, plus more for pan

4½ cups granulated sugar

9 egg yolks

½ cup ricotta cheese

1 tablespoon baking powder

¼ cup finely ground pistachios

Grated zest of 1 orange

¼ cup amaretto

4 egg whites

STRAWBERRY-LEMON COMPOTE

1 cup sugar

1 cup water

1 pound strawberries, hulled

Zest of 2 lemons

CANDIED PISTACHIOS

2 cups pistachios, shelled

1 cup confectioners' sugar

1 tablespoon grapeseed or canola oil

1 cup granulated sugar

🕐 Prep time: 1 hour, 30 minutes

🖥 Season 5, Episode 2

🔪 Elimination Challenge:
Create a New American lunch dish for fifty chefs who auditioned for *Top Chef*.

POUND CAKE RATIO

1 part butter: 1 part sugar: 1 part egg: 1 part flour

Pound cakes are so-called because they were originally made with a pound each of butter, sugar, eggs, and flour. This ratio has given way to modern recipes. A pound cake should be dense and moist; adding a dairy ingredient such as yogurt, crème fraîche, or, in this case, ricotta, tends to lighten the cake and adds a nice creamy flavor.

SERVES 10 TO 12

FOR THE POUND CAKE: Preheat the oven to 375°F. Butter, then flour a 10-inch spring-form pan. In the bowl of a stand mixer fitted with the paddle attachment, cream together the butter and granulated sugar until light and fluffy. On medium speed, add the egg yolks one at a time, beating after each addition until well incorporated. Reduce the speed to low, add the ricotta cheese, flour, and baking powder, and mix until well combined. Mix in the pistachios, orange zest, and amaretto.

In a separate bowl, whisk the egg whites to soft peaks. Gently fold the egg whites into the cake batter. Transfer the batter to the prepared pan and bake until a cake tester inserted in the center comes out clean, about 40 minutes. Let cool on a rack.

FOR THE STRAWBERRY-LEMON COMPOTE In a medium saucepan, combine the sugar and water and cook over medium-low heat until the sugar dissolves and the mixture has a syrupy consistency. Add the strawberries and lemon zest and cook down the fruit for 1 hour. Remove from the heat and let cool slightly.

Transfer the strawberry mixture to a blender and purée until smooth. Set aside.

FOR THE CANDIED PISTACHIOS: Toss the nuts in a large bowl with the confectioners' sugar. In a large skillet, heat the oil over medium-high heat and fry the pistachios until golden brown, shaking the skillet frequently to prevent the nuts from burning. Remove from the heat, add the granulated sugar, and toss the nuts until coated.

To serve, place a slice of cake on each dessert plate and drizzle with the compote. Garnish each plate with candied pistachios.

ASH AND ASHLEY'S CHOCOLATE-PEANUT BUTTER BREAD PUDDING

5 eggs

1 cup honey

1½ cups heavy cream

½ loaf brioche, preferably day old, cut into bite-sized cubes

1 cup semisweet chocolate chips

Butter for greasing

1 cup sweetened condensed milk

1½ cups creamy peanut butter

SERVES 6

Whisk together the eggs and honey until fluffy and pale in color.

In a medium saucepan, warm 1 cup of the cream over medium heat until bubbles form on the surface. Reduce the heat to low. Temper the egg mixture by adding about ¼ cup of the hot cream to the egg mixture while whisking constantly to prevent curdling. Pour the warmed egg mixture into the saucepan of cream, whisking until thickened, about 5 minutes. Remove from the heat.

In a large bowl, combine the custard and bread cubes. Stir in the chocolate chips. Let stand to allow the bread to absorb the custard, at least 30 minutes at room temperature and up to overnight in the refrigerator.

Preheat the oven to 350°F. Butter an 8-inch square baking pan.

Pour the bread mixture into the prepared pan. Fit the baking pan into a roasting pan, and pour hot tap water into the roasting pan to come halfway up the sides of the pudding pan. Bake until a knife inserted in the center of the pudding comes out clean, 40 to 45 minutes. Remove the pudding from the oven and let cool for at least 1 hour before serving.

While the bread pudding is baking, combine the remaining ½ cup cream and the condensed milk in a medium saucepan over medium heat. When the mixture bubbles, reduce the heat to low, whisk in the peanut butter, and stir until smooth. Remove from the heat.

To serve, spoon the peanut butter sauce onto each plate. Top with a slice of bread pudding and additional sauce.

🕐 **Prep time:** 45 minutes, plus baking

🖥 **Season 6, Episode 3**

✎ **Elimination Challenge:** Create a dish to serve 300 airmen using only the supplies and equipment from a mess hall.

HOW TO MAKE

hard sauce

This pudding was made for a military luncheon, with families in tow, which made peanut butter sauce an appropriate accompaniment. At home you're free to use the hard stuff: melt a stick of butter in a small saucepan; gradually whisk in 1 cup sugar until thickened. Remove from the heat and slowly add ½ cup whiskey or bourbon. Serve warm over the bread pudding.

TOP TATTOO

Chefs like tattoos; it's part of the whole rebel-rock star image of someone who works nights and will never, ever sit behind a desk. Every season has seen its share of tatted limbs. In Season 5, Jamie and Eugene stood out for their extensive body art. Even Stephanie, low-key winner of Season 4, had some ink. But Season 6 chefs took the cake for having by far the most collective ink. Perhaps the most artistically enhanced chef ever to cook on *Top Chef*, Ashley Merriman talks about her tattoos and dishes on the impressive body art of her Season 6 castmates.

WHEN DID YOU GET YOUR FIRST TATTOO AND WHAT WAS IT?
I got my first tattoo the minute I was legally able to get it—pretty much the day I turned eighteen. It was a terribly done little blob on my ankle. When I was much younger, I tried to go into tattoo shops and get a Guns N' Roses tattoo. They politely declined, fortunately for me.

IS THERE SPECIAL CONNECTION BETWEEN CHEFS AND TATTOOS?
Chefs don't have to go into office jobs every day where tattoos might be frowned upon, so perhaps that's why there are a lot of chefs out there with tattoos.

WHAT TATTOO DO YOU WANT TO GET NEXT?
I'd like to get a tattoo for my dog, Oni, who was, sadly, stolen from me. It's going to be on my ribs: a black octopus with one white eyelash with the word "tender." She was a gentle giant, a great Dane, and the most tender dog ever. I miss her very much.

TELL US ABOUT YOUR TATTOOS.
I got this tattoo in honor of my family. It's done by one of my favorite artists, Tom Yak. And no, it's not a Bob Seger reference.

This is on my chest and says "Hope and Anchor." It took a long time to finish because after the first sitting I didn't want to go back again. The chest area hurts like crazy!

I got the heart tattoo many years ago with my best friend at the time. I got the "Little Queen" (a lyric from a Heart song) one about a year ago for my own Little Queen.

This one takes up the upper half of my back and is also done by Tom Yak. I love flowers and birds and have a ton of tattoos of them.

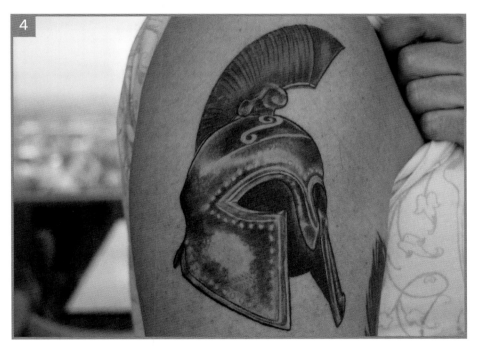

1. ELI

Everyone has to have a first tattoo. Mine is a black blob on my ankle a lot like this one. Eli should cover his up with Banyuls vinegar—one of his favorite ingredients!

2. LAURINE

Laurine's nickname in the house was Sunshine, so I like this tattoo for her. It works and looks great.

3. JESSE

I love Jesse's meat tattoo because it's a great chef tattoo without being too heavy-handed. I'm looking forward to seeing the dragon on her other leg done.

4. MIKE I.

Mike I. has a lot of incredible work. I love this tattoo and think the color and shading are incredible.

5. MATTIN

Mattin's got a few tattoos and loves to show them off in the hot tub while he's swinging his shirt over his head.

6. MICHAEL V.

Michael V. has some of the best work in the house. This is a nice chef-y tattoo, and I love the placement. Also, the sleeve one is incredible, as is the cross on his arm.

STEPHANIE'S GORGONZOLA CHEESECAKE

WINNER!

GORGONZOLA CHEESECAKE

3/4 cup heavy cream

2 ounces gorgonzola cheese

1 1/2 cups (12 ounces) cream cheese, at room temperature

2 egg yolks, at room temperature

1 tablespoon brown sugar

CONCORD GRAPE SAUCE

2 cups Concord grapes, or 2 cups unsweetened Concord grape juice

1 tablespoon balsamic vinegar

1 tablespoon water

WALNUT CRUMBLE

Canola oil for greasing (optional)

2 cups sugar

2 tablespoons water

2 tablespoons unsalted butter

2 cups chopped walnuts

SERVES 8

FOR THE GORGONZOLA CHEESECAKE: Preheat the oven to 350°F.

In a medium bowl, combine the heavy cream and gorgonzola. Place over (not touching) simmering water in a saucepan and heat, stirring occasionally, until smooth. Set aside to cool.

In the bowl of a stand mixer fitted with the paddle attachment, beat together the cream cheese, egg yolks, brown sugar, and gorgonzola mixture just until combined. Divide the mixture among eight 4-ounce ramekins and place the ramekins in a shallow roasting pan. Pour hot water 1/4 inch deep into the pan, and cover the pan with aluminum foil. Bake until the cheesecakes are just set but still jiggly in the center, about 30 minutes. Remove the ramekins from the water bath and let cool.

FOR THE CONCORD GRAPE SAUCE: In a medium nonreactive pot, combine the Concord grapes with the balsamic vinegar and water over medium-high heat. Cook until the liquid reduces by one-half, about 30 minutes. Transfer the grapes to a blender or food processor and process until smooth. Strain the sauce through a fine-mesh sieve and set aside.

FOR THE WALNUT CRUMBLE: Line a baking sheet with a Silpat or oil it well. In a heavy-bottomed medium saucepan, combine the sugar and water and bring to a gentle boil over medium-high heat. As the sugar begins to caramelize, lightly swirl the pan and continue to cook until the sugar turns a rich golden brown. Remove from the heat and stir in the butter and walnuts. Pour the caramel onto the prepared baking sheet, spreading it evenly, and let cool. Break into bite-sized pieces. Set aside.

To serve, use a kitchen blowtorch on the bottom of each ramekin to loosen the cheesecake, then invert onto a small plate to unmold. Spoon a little grape sauce onto each dessert plate and place a cheesecake alongside. Top with walnut crumble.

Prep time: 45 minutes

Season 4, Episode 11

Elimination Challenge: Restaurant Wars—open a restaurant for dinner service.

ABOUT A TECHNIQUE

a nice warm bath

Cheesecakes, like other custards, are usually cooked in a water bath (also called a bain-marie) because they need to bake slowly in a moist environment and at an even temperature. This ensures that the inside just cooks through without the top drying out.

NILS NOREN'S CHOCOLATE-GOAT CHEESE GANACHE

CHOCOLATE-GOAT CHEESE GANACHE

4 sheets leaf gelatin or 1 teaspoon powdered gelatin

2 cups heavy cream

8 ounces fresh goat cheese

3 1/2 tablespoons honey

2 pounds bittersweet chocolate, chopped

CARA CARA ORANGE GEL

3 1/2 cups Cara Cara orange juice

10 grams agar-agar powder

1/2 cup simple syrup

LAPSANG CREAM

4 cups heavy cream

3/4 cup Lapsang souchong tea leaves

1/4 cup simple syrup

GARNISH

8 Cara Cara oranges, supremed

1 cup shelled pistachios, chopped

SERVES 12

FOR THE CHOCOLATE-GOAT CHEESE GANACHE: In a small bowl, immerse the gelatin sheets in water just to cover until softened, 5 to 15 minutes, then squeeze out the excess. Or, sprinkle the powdered gelatin over a little water to soften, 3 to 5 minutes. Meanwhile, in a medium saucepan, bring the cream, goat cheese, and honey to a boil. Remove from the heat. Add the gelatin to the hot goat cheese–cream mixture and stir until fully dissolved. Put the chocolate in a medium bowl and pour the hot cheese mixture on top. Mix until smooth. Transfer to a shallow 9-by-13-inch baking pan and set aside.

FOR THE CARA CARA ORANGE GEL: In a medium saucepan, bring 1 3/4 cups of the orange juice to a boil with the agar-agar and simple syrup. Remove from the heat and pour the mixture into a shallow pan. Chill until set.

Transfer the orange gel to a blender with the remaining 3/4 cup orange juice and blend until smooth. Set aside.

FOR THE LAPSANG CREAM: In a medium saucepan, heat the cream to a gentle simmer over low heat and add the tea. Remove from heat and let the cream cool. Chill the infused cream in the refrigerator for 1 hour. Strain the cream into the bowl of a stand mixer fitted with the whisk attachment and whip on moderate speed until the cream thickens. Gradually add the simple syrup and whip on high speed until soft peaks form. Or, pour the strained cream into an iSi cream whipper and whip to soft peaks according to the manufacturer's instructions. Set aside.

To serve, slice the ganache into 24 triangles. Place 2 pieces of ganache on each plate. Top with a spoonful of the orange gel and sprinkle the dessert with the orange segments and pistachios.

Prep time: 2 hours, plus chilling

Top Chef Masters,
Season 1, Episode 5

Elimination Challenge:
Create a mini appetizer, entrée, and dessert for 100 people.

ABOUT AN INGREDIENT

agar-agar

Derived from seaweed, agar-agar is a thickener and gelling agent. It has long been used as a common ingredient in Japanese desserts and also as a thickener in many commercial foods in the United States. More recently, the molecular gastronomy movement has embraced it as a fast-acting (and vegetarian) alternative to gelatin. Here, Nils Noren uses it to make his orange gel; Hector also employed agar-agar to create the ingenious mango and cilantro-mint "pearls" in his Tofu Ceviche (page 128).

LAURINE'S BACON DOUGHNUTS

DOUGHNUTS

1¼ cups all-purpose flour

1½ teaspoons baking powder

¼ teaspoon baking soda

¼ teaspoon ground cinnamon

¼ teaspoon salt

1 egg

½ cup buttermilk

2 tablespoons bacon fat or melted butter

3 slices apple wood–smoked bacon, cooked until crisp and chopped (fat reserved for batter)

CHOCOLATE SAUCE

⅓ cup water

4 ounces 58-percent cacao bittersweet chocolate, chopped

1 tablespoon light corn syrup

DOUGHNUT COATING

½ teaspoon superfine sugar

½ teaspoon ground cinnamon

½ teaspoon ground ginger

¼ teaspoon freshly ground pepper

Pinch of salt

Canola oil for deep-frying

Beer Sauce (below)

1 slice apple wood–smoked bacon, cooked until crisp

MAKES 20 DOUGHNUT HOLES

FOR THE DOUGHNUTS: Sift the flour, baking powder, baking soda, cinnamon, and salt together into a large bowl. In a separate bowl, combine the egg, buttermilk, and bacon fat. Fold the wet ingredients into the dry ingredients and stir in the chopped bacon until well incorporated. Let the batter rest for 30 minutes.

FOR THE CHOCOLATE SAUCE: In a saucepan, bring the water to boil over medium-high heat. Add the chocolate and corn syrup and whisk until smooth. Remove from the heat and set aside.

FOR THE DOUGHNUT COATING: Sift the superfine sugar, cinnamon, ginger, pepper, and salt together into a medium bowl and set aside.

Pour 3 to 4 inches of oil into a deep, heavy-bottomed pot or Dutch oven and heat to 340°F on a deep-frying thermometer. Line a baking sheet with paper towels. Working in batches, drop heaping tablespoons of the doughnut batter into the hot oil and fry, turning once, until golden on all sides, about 2 minutes. Remove the doughnuts with a slotted spoon and drain on the paper towels. Toss the doughnuts in the spice mixture and set aside.

To serve, place the doughnuts on a plate and serve the chocolate and beer sauces on the side. Garnish with an additional slice of bacon, if desired.

Prep time: 30 minutes

Season 6, Episode 1

Elimination Challenge: Cook a dish based on one of your personal vices.

HOW TO MAKE

beer sauce

2 cups fruit lambic ale, such as kriek, framboise, or pomme

1 cup apple juice

½ cup sour-style Belgian beer, such as Rodenbach Grand Cru

1 cinnamon stick

1 cardamom pod

2 tablespoons unsalted butter

In a large saucepan, combine all the ingredients except the butter over medium-low heat. Reduce to a thick syrup, about 25 minutes, stirring minimally. Remove from the heat, remove the cinnamon stick and cardamom pod, and whisk in the butter to finish.

OUTTAKES

....

1. Host Padma Lakshmi and Chef and head judge Tom Colicchio

2. Season 4 winner Stephanie

3. Season 5 runner-up Carla

4. Carla demonstrates her majorette skills with fellow Season 5 chef'testants Hosea, Fabio, and Stefan, and judge Toby Young (center).

5. The cast of Season 6 goes in for a huddle (from left: Robin, Bryan, Jennifer C., Mike I., Michael V., Kevin, and Eli).

6. Season 4 chef'testant Antonia

7. Season 3 chef'testant C.J.

8. Season 2 runner-up Marcel

9. Host Padma Lakshmi

MENUS

INDEX

ACKNOWLEDGMENTS

Top Chef has become a phenomenon. Each new season and iteration of the show proves that America loves a cooking competition, and every season the culinary sophistication of the audience grows broader and deeper. Since our first two cookbooks (*Top Chef: The Cookbook and Top Chef: The Quickfire Cookbook*), an extraordinary roster of guest chefs and celebrities evolved into a celebration of chefs at the pinnacle of the craft: *Top Chef Masters*. Our incomparable panel of judges act as the ballast of the show, and the chef'testants themselves have evolved into a who's who of up-and-coming cooks from around the country and the world. The time is ripe to teach the foundations of every great chef to every person who adores *Top Chef*.

The show is a competition, and we emphasize the drama and tension that happens naturally when talented young chefs battle it out to get to the top. But after watching and being entertained, viewers are also inspired to push themselves further in the kitchen, to try new ingredients and techniques, and maybe even to enter the culinary profession. *Top Chef* has brought formerly wonky culinary terms like *mise en place*, *brunoise*, and *gastrique* into the mainstream, and has become a true showcase for exciting global ingredients and innovative cooking. This book celebrates the culinary phenomenon that the show has become, and that's something we can all be proud of.

— Lauren Zalaznick
President, NBC Universal Women & Lifestyle Entertainment Networks

Thanks to Tom Colicchio, Padma Lakshmi, Gail Simmons, and Toby Young.

Thanks to the team at Bravo Media: Frances Berwick, Cameron Blanchard, Victoria Brody, Andrew Cohen, Sarah Conrad, Courtney Fleischman, Johanna Fuentes, Lauren McCollester, Kate Pappa, Suzanne Park, Dave Serwatka, Ellen Stone, Trez Thomas, Jennifer Turner, and Andrew Ulanoff.

Thanks to the team at Magical Elves: Doneen Arquines, Rich Buhrman, Liz Cook, Dan Cutforth, Bill Egle, Gayle Gawlowski, Chi Kephart, Jane Lipsitz, Shauna Minoprio, Molly O'Rourke, Erin Rott, Nan Strait, Andrew Wallace, and Webb Weiman.

Thanks to the *Top Chef Masters* chefs and *Top Chef* guest judges who participated in this book: Rick Bayless, John Besh, Michael Chiarello, Wylie Dufresne, Hubert Keller, Anita Lo, Eric Ripert, and Suzanne Tracht.

Thanks to the chef'testants who participated in this book: Stephen Asprinio, Richard Blais, Jennifer Carroll, Nikki Cascone, Ariane Duarte, Lisa Fernandes, Kevin Gillespie, Carla Hall, Hung Huynh, Mike Isabella, Stephanie Izard, Eli Kirshtein, Jamie Lauren, Spike Mendelsohn, Ashley Merriman, Jeff McInnis, Stefan Richter, Hosea Rosenberg, Dale Talde, Marcel Vigneron, Eugene Villiatora, Fabio Viviani, Bryan Voltaggio, Michael Voltaggio, and Lee Anne Wong.

Thanks also to the Chronicle Books team: Sarah Billingsley, Mikyla Bruder, Vanessa Dina, Anne Donnard, Catherine Grishaver, David Hawk, Lorena Jones, Ben Kasman, Jennifer Kong, Maile Marshall, Amy Nichols, Doug Ogan, Peter Perez, and Ann Spradlin.

Thanks to all our sponsors, without whom *Top Chef* would not be possible.

SOURCES

Activa

Also called "meat glue" and "transglutaminase," Activa is available online from retailers such as Amazon.com and Lepicerie.com.

Agar Agar

This seaweed-derived gelling agent can be found at Amazon.com, Bulkfoods.com, and Edenfoods.com.

Agave Nectar

The natural sweetener agar agar is sold at well-stocked supermarkets and health food stores. Find it online at Amazon.com, Agavenectar.com, Madhavasagave.com, and other outlets.

Glucose

Glucose can be purchased in paste form from any cake decorating supply store, such as www.wilton.com.

Carageenan

Also known as Irish moss, this seaweed-derived thickener and emulsifier is available from many natural foods stores, such as www.frontiercoop.com.

Soy Lecithin

This product has become much more widely available with the growth of gluten-free baking. Find it at Bobsredmill.com and Amazon.com.

Liquid Nitrogen

Liquid nitrogen canisters are available at welding supply and gas supply stores. Before purchasing, make sure you are up to speed on all safety precautions.

Xanthan Gum

This common thickener is available at many natural foods stores, and online at sites such as Bobsredmill.com and Americanspice.com.

TABLE OF EQUIVALENTS

The exact equivalents in the following tables have been rounded for convenience.

LIQUID/DRY MEASURES

U.S.	METRIC
1/4 teaspoon	1.25 milliliters
1/2 teaspoon	2.5 milliliters
1 teaspoon	5 milliliters
1 tablespoon (3 teaspoons)	15 milliliters
1 fluid ounce (2 tablespoons)	30 milliliters
1/4 cup	60 milliliters
1/3 cup	80 milliliters
1/2 cup	120 milliliters
1 cup	240 milliliters
1 pint (2 cups)	480 milliliters
1 quart (4 cups, 32 ounces)	960 milliliters
1 gallon (4 quarts)	3.84 liters
1 ounce (by weight)	28 grams
1 pound	454 grams
2.2 pounds	1 kilogram

LENGTH

U.S.	METRIC
1/8 inch	3 millimeters
1/4 inch	6 millimeters
1/2 inch	12 millimeters
1 inch	2.5 centimeters

OVEN TEMPERATURE

FAHRENHEIT	CELSIUS	GAS
250	120	1/2
275	140	1
300	150	2
325	160	3
350	180	4
375	190	5
400	200	6
425	220	7
450	230	8
475	240	9
500	260	10

Also available now, other best-selling titles by the creators of *Top Chef:*

Top Chef: The Cookbook

More than 100 recipes and tips, plus original interviews and behind-the-scenes stories from Bravo's hit show.

978-0-8118-7347-5

$29.95 hc

A *NEW YORK TIMES* BEST-SELLER!

Top Chef Quickfire Challenge Game

Relive favorite Top Chef *moments by answering trivia questions about the contestants, the judges, and the food.*

978-0-8118-6994-2

$19.95 box with trivia cards, game boards, and game pieces

Top Chef: The Quickfire Cookbook

Re-create the Quickfire Challenge—the most exciting part of Bravo's Top Chef— *anytime, anywhere!*

978-0-8118-7082-5

$29.95 hc

A *NEW YORK TIMES* BEST-SELLER!